T0366001

WAIT, LISTEN, RECORD

HABAKKUK 2:1-3

Jessie Schlaser

Order this book online at www.trafford.com
or email orders@trafford.com

Most Trafford titles are also available at major online book retailers.

Print information available on the last page.

ISBN: 978-1-6987-0959-8 (sc)
ISBN: 978-1-6987-0958-1 (e)

Scripture quotations taken from the Holy Bible, New International Version®.
NIV®. Copyright © 1973, 1978, 1984 by International Bible Society. Used
by permission of Zondervan. All rights reserved. [Biblica]¨

Trafford rev. 09/30/2021

 www.trafford.com
North America & international
toll-free: 844-688-6899 (USA & Canada)
fax: 812 355 4082

SET UP BOOK

1 - CHAPTERS – YEARS (1994 through 2010)
2 - SUBTITLES – DATE: <u>XXXXXX</u> title
3 - END EACH YEAR WITH A SPECIAL MESSAGE: ARTICLE, POEM, ETC.
4 - <u>ALL NAMES TO BE CHANGED TO PROTECT THE INNOCENT.</u> SOME ARE DECEASED, SOME ACQUAINTANCES, FRIENDS AND FAMILY.

1 - TESTIMONY OF FREDS MAJOR HEART ATTACK, <u>NAME OK</u>
2 - BIBLE REFERENCES ARE FROM NKJ AND OR NIV

DEDICATE BOOK TO MY DAUGHTER ALICE FORD

I really didn't start serving the lord until 1980.

My mother passed away and I came back home to astoria to settle the estate. Did not plan on staying on after that right off I met a wonderful women that took me under her arm… and led me back to the church. Until then I had not attended church on a regular bases as my husband was not a christian and refused to attend any church at that time.

This new friend (sister in the lord) taught and showed me what it meant and how to serve God the way he wanted us to, in a goldy manner and not through self glory but to always do it in his glory. I learned how to see people as Jesus sees the. Not by their exterior or their life styles but by their hearts, and how I could help them learn and grow in the lord and at the same time God was showing and teaching me how to walk the talk

HEAR MY CALL

I saw in the east as far as one could see—fields of white ripe grain waiting to be harvested. Their heads turning ever which way. To the west as far as one could see—the deserts are alive with color, the flowers in full bloom like a rainbow in all her glorious vibrant colors, nodding their heads, waiting to be picked, "yes", it's time; seed pods ready to burst open.

Jesus hovering over, looking down without stretched arms, calling; come hither my children; the fields are ready for harvest—the flowers are pregnant, ready to give birth—the time is now before the darkness covers over all the earth. Tears streaming down his cheeks as he continues to call out. Hurry my children!

The sky is filled with angels, all clothed in white, waiting, waiting to receive us into the arms of Jesus!

He is coming for his bride!

A MAGNIFICENT CROWN

I ask the lord today, if my gathering of used bibles was really doing some good. I was wondering if most was getting to a place and then just sitting in a corner or being tossed aside and forgotten, and really going nowhere in the end. Are hearts really being reached? Are they getting to the lost and fallen?

Then to my amazement this is what the lord showed me.

A large crown 16-18 inches across and about 12 inches high. It was beautiful—all shimmery and sparkly. Had many beautiful gem-stones— all sizes, shapes and colors and kinds I've never seen before. They all sparkled, almost in a blinding way as the sun shown down upon it. As I looked closer I could see many open, empty places. My thoughts were—the craftsman hasn't finished with it yet and God was just letting me get a glimpse of his, handiwork, ahead of time.

Then he said; the empty places you see are: some of the people are in the process of turning their lives around, but totally haven't given it all to me. But it's on the way. While other empty places are for those yet to come into their place of salvation and the kingdom, they haven't heard about me yet. This is your crown and yours alone.

Wow! Only God can give answers like that.

ANGEL OF THE LORD

While walking down the sidewalk by the Liberty Theater—window shopping to kill some time, before my next visitation; I noticed a well-dressed, gentleman sitting on a milk stool, by the middle pillar of the store front, by the door of the dress shop. He was middle aged, with a warm smile, clean shaven, (well-groomed to be exact) and a kind loving face. I thought he was just resting there and waiting for someone. As I approached him, he held out his hand and ask for some small change. (I was so surprised to hear that from such a well- dressed person, besides this sort of thing is very unusual here. These kind of beggars are really street people; dirty scrounge and usually burned out on drugs or alcohol) I couldn't believe what I was seeing. I gave a quick NO answer and hurried on to cross the street before the light turned red. BUT as soon as I said no, I knew I did it wrong, as I couldn't look him in the eye while saying it. (clue #1) As I continued to cross the street the guilt really hit me so I quickly turned to go back just before reaching the curb. I hurried back to where the man was sitting to give him what money I had which was only a dollar at that time. I didn't want to dig through to find any small change that I might have.

But to my amazement the man was gone, stool and all. I looked everywhere, in all the stores in that area which are but very few, and really nothing a man would be shopping in, no food places or even any beer taverns. I looked and ask questions, no one had seen anything. I even ask the lady of the dress shop where he was sitting, by her, in her doorway. I ask her if she had seen which way he had gone, as she was standing there while he was sitting there, so she surely saw something. She said no that she hadn't seen anyone. I said the man that was sitting right here by your door. She said that there was no one there by my door. I again told her, there was, and surely she must have seen him when he got up to leave at least. She again informed me there was no one sitting by her door, I have been here the whole time and I would know if someone was sitting by my door. My reply was OOOH MY. I continued to look, as I was returning to my car. Now it seems more important than ever to find this man.

Finally, a little voice in my head convinced me that it was an angel from God, and I failed the test. I knew I had to get to a church and get before God and ask forgiveness for my stupid blunder. Being fairly late in the afternoon I knew my church would be closed by this time, so where can I go, that there still may be someone there? I went to the First Christian Church on 11th street. As I felt all right there. That is where I went to church in my teens and accepted the Lord in my life and I was married in that church also. So I felt at home there even though I wouldn't know this pastor.

I tried the door, and it was locked—now where do I go, I really didn't want to go to the Catholic Church, but I would if I couldn't find another. But suddenly the door opened and the young pastor asks me what I wanted? I told him all I wanted was to use the sanctuary for a short time. When I finished I had to go back out through the Pastor's office door. He was sitting there studying for his Sunday service. I told him of my experience and why I wanted to use the altar. His first words were "you blew it didn't you? That was an angel from God, maybe He had a word for you. It seems strange that you should drop in here at this very time, I am preparing a sermon on visiting angels". He had told me who but I don't remember.

I really didn't need conformation that I had blown it, I already knew that quite clearly.

When I returned home there was a letter from a missionary that was collecting $15.00 to send a food box to a family in Russia. Josh McDowell ministries. At that point we hadn't received much literature from them. I took that, as God was giving me another chance to prove my faith and if, I really was sorry.

I sent the money off in the next mail, and then, I felt forgiven,

We never know when that person we helped, however small it seemed, may have been sent by the Lord. He does send angels in disguise

GOD'S GIFT TO MANKIND

Lord, my creator-your awesomeness is far beyond my comprehension. You spoke the word and it was created. You breathed upon it and it became a living thing. You created the heavens and the earth.

You made the rains and the waters became rivers and oceans. You raised the land and formed the mountains, craters and formed caverns and lakes upon and beneath the land surface to assure us of pure waters that we might not thirst. You spoke and filled the waters with living food-even formed the crawlers and skimmers to clean the waters. Creatures and swimmers-to numerous to name. Many are hidden and unknown to us, but you know their every name and fill their needs also.

The fowl of the air, some to clean the edges and surfaces of the waters. Then there are those that will feed upon the frogs and minnows in the waters. The scavengers that we call pests all to manicure our landscapes. You know the ugly ones.

The tides to clean out the rubbish that we humans toss aside; and flush away the fallen debris along the banks of the streams and rivers. You bring fresh food for the creatures that feed on the beaches and rocky shores. Of our sea shores.

The torrential rains to clean the debris from within the trees, which in turn nourish the soil with nutrition for the ground cover. You fill the streams, the lakes, the ponds, the swamps: to make sure all your living things have sufficient shelter and food supply: that all things may live.

The birds of the air, with their wings out-stretched-gliding with grace and ease: or soaring with great speed and determination, all using the winds as their guide. They sing and dance their praises to their creator all mighty God. It is sweet music to our souls. They flutter and show off their beautiful coats of many colors. Each with its own special gifting you gave to them freely.

Oh Lord you saw to it to give to man fishes of the sea, animals of the land and fowl to nourish our bodies: and your living word to feed our souls. You double checked to make sure there was plenty to feed all the living creatures upon and within the earth. You didn't miss a thing everything is just perfect. We call that your survival plan, you call it creation.

You give us the winds. Some to cool our bodies, some to cleanse the trees and sweep clean the ground. The winds bring the clouds over to water the earth and give us water for our bodies that gives us life and sustains all living matter. Sometimes the winds that over power us is your loving spirit throwing your arms and everlasting love over us. And sometimes through the misty clouds that drift in the winds bring us a glimpse of your artists palette with a beautiful rainbow of awesome colors and with it telling us the story of the flood in the days of Noah. That you will never destroy the world again by flood.

As we stand and look around us: everywhere we look, we can see your wonderful works. From the tiniest insect to the most majestic mammoth mountain. We cannot comprehend your awesome creativeness. And the people. From the twelve tribes of Israel, we look at the many colors of skin: the many nationalities, the many languages. Only you lord can do such a marvel. How different each individual is, each person has his or her own giftings: our own individualities, and personalities. You created each one of us special and different from any other person. You made me, you formed me, you knew me before I was ever formed in my mother's womb.

I TOLD YA-SO

I crushed two vertebras in my upper spine during some physical exercise, (weight lifting class). After two weeks of excruciating pain I went to the Doctor and the x-rays confirmed there were two crushed ones. they informed me it would be 3-6 months before they would be healed enough for the pain to subside and be free of a specialist for a brace to keep me from using my back so it could heal, knowing I wasn't about to lay around and do nothing. I told both Doctors; "no way, one month is all you get, that's all the time you get; I got things to do, places to go, and people to see." You just don't talk to a Doctor that way, they know best and how things work. He kept insisting I was being a little ridiculous in my thinking. I repeated it—one month it will be healed completely.

He still gave me an appointment to come back in a month's time for a check to see how well it is healing. When the month's appointment came around, I kept it at which time more x-rays and to receive instructions for therapy and exercises to strengthen the muscles. While waiting for the x-rays to come back to the Doctor again: I informed them it was all healed now. And again he would patiently explain to me that I just don't understand fully but I'm saying it is all healed. You will see when you read the x-rays.

Now for show and tell time. The Doctor pops the x-ray film on the screen and looks and looks some more and does a few hmmmms. Do you remember which ones it was, I see some damaged ones here but there is no indication of any swelling or irritation. I don't quite understand maybe the technician didn't get the right angle and missed it. I guess if it doesn't hurt you any more it must be all right. He poked and prodded some more with no pain so he had to concede.

I told you it would be healed in a month's time. The Lord did it! Well I hear those sort of things happen sometimes.

I was then dismissed and didn't need to return unless I had further problems with it. ISN'T GOD GOOD?

I had to stop the physical exercises as it was all weights. I still had bad backaches when I would over-do—But God healed that too. The only problem I have now—is I can't lift over 20 pounds without it causing pain and letting me know that's enough. My main pain is my EGO, now that hurts. I'm used to doing it myself; move it, push it, carry it, what ever it took. I find there is a lot of things I can no longer do. My pride is really bent out of shape, but I really have no choice in the matter; now do I.

SATAN ATTACK

Last night I was awakened with the vision of Satan in silhouette' form and his helping demons marching toward me, very slowly. With one stronger than the rest, leading out front. I tried to shake it off as a bad dream. They just kept coming. I got up and walked around, I thought if I got wide awake it would go away. I went back to bed, I could still see them very clearly. I couldn't go to sleep, they just kept coming, very slowly. I jumped out of bed they continued to come, closer and closer; they wouldn't stop or go away. I then realized this is not a dream, this is the real thing. I began rebuking them emphatically. They fled immediately. I thanked God for the power of the Holy Spirit.

I had spent about three months researching books written by other ministries and researching scriptures; on the workings of the cults and occults. What Satan can and cannot do.

I was doing this because of the activities going on in and around our community. Also the prison I write to is asking for answers as there seem to be satanic activity picking up in the prison. I was trying to keep the covering of God and into the word the whole time as I know how this kind of thing can influence and infilter the subconscious mind. So I was very aware of what I was doing and how dangerous this study was. I kept in prayer and studying the word with it.

I felt strong enough in the Lord that I could discern any evil that Satan would throw my way, As "He that is in me is greater than he that is in the world." I knew that I had the Lord Jesus Christ and this was a study to learn the tricks of the evil one. I also knew Satan would not like me to find out his ways. So I had to be aware at all times. I guess Satan was going to try to show me differently.

Just reading Satanic material is very dangerous, it will infiltrate the subconscious mind. Satan will use it and continually bring it to the surface; and will deceive you by convincing you it is O.K. to continue to read and participate in little things. That is how he traps you, before you know it you are participating in more and more 'little' things that seem so harmless.

If you have participated in any games of witch-craft or satanic nature get on your knees and ask God to forgive you and clean that past out before it gets a bigger hold on you. Even so innocent appearing can be so devastating in our lives, Satan jumps on every opening he finds to lure us away from salvation, and God.

STANDING ALONE

When you left the Lord standing alone
and betrayed those that Love you,
you pierced our hearts with no misgiving.
As we watched you sink deeper and deeper
into the quick-sands of the desolate,
our hearts were quickened as pierced with a sword.
Even so you were never alone,
for the tears we shed, to lift you from the mire,
the Lord too stood by- watched and wept.
The Loving hand is still out stretched
to be received and lift you back to higher ground,
I am always with you, I will never forsake you.
For by Grace ye are saved through faith;
and that not of yourself. It is the Gift if God.
He will lift you higher than you've ever known.
This is my song, this is my story,
praising the Lord the live long day;
that one day you will receive your crown
and live in the land of Glory by the River of Life.

KS

MY ANOINTING

I got it! I got it! I got it! Hallelujah, I got it, BIG time. I got it all! I was also delivered of all those past hurts. It started when we went to another church to hear a speaker from another area speak on the working of the Holy Spirit. March 1, the first night when they called "every one" to come and be prayed for. While I was down the Holy Spirit covered me with a blanket, was about 4 to 5 inches thick. Light gray and very, very soft. I remember thinking to my self, while people were stepping over me; "don't step on my blanket". I could see it and feel of it. It seemed to hang around the rest of the week, but not too strong, to my consciousness, but I knew it was still there if I stopped and thought about it.

Sunday morning as I entered the church sanctuary it came back just as strong as it was that first night. As the praise and worship went on, it got stronger and began to press into me to the point that it was pushing me back into my seat.

Sunday evening service it wrapped around me and was so strong as it was that first night. As the praise and worship went on, it got stronger and began to press into me to the point that it was pushing me back into my seat.

The next morning it was snugly wrapped around me. As I began my day it became tighter, and the anointing became heavier. I knew God was doing something tremendous. I've known for quite awhile that he was doing a work in me getting me ready for something great. I went on my business of the day, I had gone into town to do some things I needed to do. I had to get some copies made of some scripture work I had done for someone, and while doing that people were looking at me and smiling and speaking, I felt like a 10000 watt light bulb, and was beginning to have trouble keeping from crying as the anointing was getting stronger. I had another stop to do that I needed for the next day, as I knew I wouldn't have time to get it done, between my people stops. I went on into this used book store to get a poetry book, as I read to some elderly people in an adult foster home. And the one I had wasn't very good. While in there I began to tremble and started crying, I just couldn't hold it back any longer, by this time the anointing was so heavy I was having trouble staying on my feet, too

I know the Angels in Heaven are rejoicing the clerk asked me if I was alright. I said yes, and I was hurrying to get done and out of there. Again she asks me if I was OK. I told her yes, I'm just having trouble keeping my composure as the Holy Spirit is upon me. Well you guessed it, she looked at me as though I was high on something, and hurried a little faster to see I got out of there. On my way out she said "I hope what ever is on you goes away real soon." I couldn't help but chuckle at that and think, oh how much you are missing out on.

I headed to my car, I knew I had to get to church so the pastor could pray for me. Ten miles away, seemed like twenty. The closer I got to the church, harder I cried the heavier the anointing became. I barely made it in the church door, then I really got hit hard with the Holy Spirit, got to Pastor's office, and he wasn't there. I started back towards the door and the pastor's wife came and asks what I needed to see pastor for. By this time all I could say was, I need prayer, she thought something terrible had happened, when she got close to me, she said what is happening to you? I said the Holy Spirit is upon me. She reached out to take my hand and, that was it, I fell in a heap and the Holy Spirit went to work. As she prayed I could feel being delivered of things. All those hurts just floated out.

After about an hour she was able to get me out of the foyer and into the sanctuary to the altar, and I spent a lot more time under the power of the Holy Spirit. The anointing stayed on me into the next day. That same night while watching Binny Hinn I received again, that was an emotional healing. It was a grand day.

I feel really washed out, but I'm just floating, I don't even feel real to myself.

I wouldn't give back those two hours for anything in the whole wide world. I am expecting the unexpected.

I don't know just what all I really got, I do know that when ever, what ever I need, it will be right there, I'm sure I will be amazed and surprised many times by what the Holy Spirit will be doing through me. I know that I know, I got my anointing for my ministry. Now when those hurting people ask for prayer, things will react. Thank you all so much for your fervent prayers. I know they all had a part in the end result. Several at church were also praying for me. I can't thank you enough. I praise God and give him all the glory.

DEEP DEPRESSION

I felt lonely and depressed. As days went on I just went deeper into depression.— I didn't want to see or be around anyone. I wanted to drop all my ministering to others—drop church—drop God; everything and everybody. I would have left home if I had any place to go and be alone. I wouldn't participate in church—I rebelled at anything. I felt like I was down in a pit. Cold dark deep pit. I could see the bottom, it was always about two feet away from my feet. I just kept going deeper and deeper—I could see out and see the light at the top. It kept going through my mind of Joseph being thrown into the pit by his brothers. (gen 37:18-30)

The farther I fell into the pit the darker it became. Although the light at the top remained the same. I knew someone would come by and help me out.

I could never touch bottom it just seemed to stay the same distance from me and moved down as I moved down.

This went on about three weeks, I just kept slipping deeper into the pit. I wouldn't study the word, I wouldn't pray,—just continued to feel sorry for myself. Finally, I decided this has gone far enough I'm not getting anywhere, just pleasing the devil. I have to pull myself out of this or I'm going to have a mental breakdown, this is not right, this is not of God.

So I started praising God and asking for His help, by this time, this was very hard to do, I had fallen so far, but something kept telling me God is always there but we need to ask. So I just kept praising and asking, it got easier and easier. All at once, I started rising up; started feeling Gods presence again, and feeling better about myself and wanting to get back to ministering to my people in the nursing home. But I had to get God back into the action and not just do it to be doing it. It was hard the first week—but I started climbing out of that depression faster and faster. The light became brighter and brighter and all of a sudden after praising and worshipping and listening to Christian tapes—I was totally free once again.

Later---

Each time I get depressed now, it is easier and faster getting free. As I get closer to God.

I found that other people from my church are being attacked in the same way, 'deep depressions', that one can't get out of by themselves. I learned that the next time I am attacked that I can go to a brother or sister in the Lord for help. God doesn't mean for us to fight these battles by ourselves. We are a body in Christ. Together we stand against the enemy.

July 1, 95

A MIRACLE HEALING

Bethel Camp

Camp time again. Each service is so full-filling.

Again I went up for each altar call, and was immediately filled and Blessed. One service the minister stood off and turned it all over to the Holy Spirit. Everyone was worshipping the Lord and it wasn't long the Holy Spirit fell upon everyone and down to the floor we all fell under the power.

I called my husband Friday evening after the service and told him he was missing some powerful blessings. He should get himself down here. He had decided he didn't want to go to camp this year. He said if he came it would be around noon but I don't know if I want to or not, I'll be there Sunday to take you home. I knew that he would be there by noon, whether he did or not.

The next morning (sat) was a miracle healing service. The Pastor ask everyone who had a real sickness and wanted a healing to come to the altar, about 11:30 am. He said a prayer for healing while everyone was getting to the front. As soon as I stepped to the front of the altar and raised my arms in worship the Holy Spirit came upon me full force; more power than I had ever experienced before; and down I went. I couldn't even hear the background praying, and commotion. I just felt shooting pains in my lower back. I just declared the healing of the Lord and kept thanking Him for my healing. The anointing went through me in waves, in slow motion; from head to toe.

- 18 -

When I began to get up, the auditorium was empty—there was one other lady beginning to stir with me. This was about 12:15. We were both crying and having trouble walking out of the building. I went directly to my room which was downstairs from the dining room. I didn't want to go into lunch crying uncontrollably. I had to get it together. I had just gotten into my room when the door opened and there stood my husband, he just stood there, and asks what was happening?

I told him I just had a miracle healing for my back—so we both stood in the middle of the room crying and thanking God.

I had two upper crushed vertebras; curvature of the spine; arthritis spurs in my lower back. Had been in much pain the past few months with it, the spurs especially. I have had no pain in my spine since.

About July 29, I had broken a rib, I went to the dr a week later because of the pain (Aug 5) for x-ray. They only confirmed it was broken and put on a binder. BUT the x-ray showed my spine was STRAIGHT, no curvature.

For the past five years or more, I have not been able to lay flat on my back without it hurting greatly as my spine was so curved it would hit first. NOW I can lay flat on the floor and even on an x-ray table with space between my vertebras and the surface in which I am laying upon. That's a miracle! I could not lay on a hard surface.

A DEPENDENT FRIEND

My very dear friend, now resides in an adult Foster Home. I visited and read the Word of God to her about eight years. Once a week on a regular basis we should first go out for lunch and do any errands she may need done and sometimes even go for rides sightseeing.

About five years ago she ask the Lord into her life; to be her Lord and Savior. How she changed from bitterness to love and caring about others. She preached to all her friends that came into her house, even argued with the Mormons that kept coming. Because of her age, in the 80's, she couldn't get out to witness to others. So she hit on everyone that entered her door. She was growing by leaps and bounds in the Lord.

The Lord was also teaching me; patience, understanding, tolerance; all the fruits of the Spirit but mostly patience and Love.

Sometimes when I would arrive she would be crying—as she had received another letter from a family member demanding they be in her will and was to receive such and such because they were a relative and it was owed to them. Sometimes it was a friend of long standing that would be demanding these same things or begging that she leave them several thousand dollars, and to be sure and put them in her will.

I have read some of those letters and heard some of her friends say these things to her in an angry and demanding voice.

At one time my friend lived a very eloquent life style, yes she is a wealthy lady. She and her husband both worked at very good paying jobs and they invested wisely. She was a collector and lover of lead-cut crystal while her husband liked antiques., But he only bought what they could use in their household. When you walked in the house you would keep your hands in your pocket so not to bump or knock anything over, she has so much beautiful crystal, everywhere.

When her eye-sight and hearing got really bad she had to stop driving and start depending on other people to escort her around. She always more than paid her way, if you would let her. Some of her "friends" began to take advantage of her generosity. They would start coming around more often and offering to take her places—but in turn would always demand a "good" meal and "gas money", for their favors.

As she became more and more dependent on others her family grew farther and farther away. They had no time for her needs so in turn they hired a friend to over-see her; to help with shopping, and tending to business affairs, etc. In the past two years all they were interested in was her business affairs and handling her money. The one that was supposed to be taking care that she had food in the house, and that she was eating properly, began playing games with her mind.

My friend hired a guy to take care of her needs. He knew what days I was with my friend and he would come by and inform us, that while we were out he filled the refrigerator and her cupboards with food and she had enough to last her for weeks., then would hurriedly leave.

Upon checking his statement, there would be nothing in the cupboards, only one gallon of milk and maybe a small carton of fresh fruit. Nothing, not even in the freezer compartment.

This went on many times that I witnessed.

This same caring person would come in and hand her an envelope and say "here is $500". And again quickly leave. When checking after he would leave, the envelope would be empty, maybe a blank piece of paper. These things went on as long as my friend remained in her home. The neighbors knew of the food games. They would call agencies trying to get help for her. My friend would call up people daily trying to get someone to go out and eat with her, she always paid the whole meal. She wouldn't have it any other way as she was a very lonely lady, and she could afford it.

My friend would question about the food and money and he always told her "she used it up already, or she had given it all away, but it was there she just don't remember,' she was imagining things."

Some of the neighbors and myself began praying that God would send someone with a pure heart to care for this ladies needs.

Another friend of ours, would come in and tell her how sick she was and that she should go to bed, she can't hardly stand-up, and let "her" take charge of things. Sometime she would shove my friend and tell her she was crazy, you shouldn't be here you should be in a hospital, Della would scream these things to her, over and over.

My friend was beginning to have hallucinations, she would talk to her dead husband or imaginary people. Sometimes she thought there were people trying to take her away. I would see this condition usually after a visit from her friend. Her friend would come see her every day. Some times she would take her to appointments.

When I would come over and find her in an anger, bitterness, emotional upset; I would talk to her, pray with her and get her to focus on Jesus. After a short time she would straighten out and all would be well again.

After we would go out for lunch we would have a Bible session. She followed along, reading aloud. If I didn't read fast enough she would read ahead of me. This would cause confusion sometimes as I'd have to get her to slow down. She couldn't learn things fast enough to suit her. She would question and understand.

Some of her friends were so against her learning anything about the Lord; they kept stealing her Bibles. One time when her Bible disappeared we prayed and ask God to put intense burning in the fingers of the one who took it so he would return it. The person, Jack returned it the next day, said he borrowed it. He was one that was against the word the most. God really answered fast that time.

After the third Bible disappeared and failed to return after three weeks I kept her Bible in my car. Her friends still kept insisting that she not let me in the house, she didn't need to know anything what was in that book, as it was written by some person that doesn't know what he is talking about.

When her little dog died about three months ago, my friend really started getting confused, but she still would come out of it when we prayed and I'd start talking to her. We still went out; and read the Bible together.

We talked and studied about heaven, dying, burial, many times, she isn't afraid of dying. She is looking forward to going home and being with her husband. He too had accepted the Lord a couple years before he died. She told me all about their baby girl they adopted and how she died.

Now she is in an adult Foster Home, and declared a full blown Alzheimer. The house-mother declaring that she has been this way for the past three years, her little book says so.

It seems that one night she went into hallucinating and was running up and down her street, The Police took her to the hospital and in there on to drugs and health care as they couldn't bring her out of her state of mind.

I go to see her as often as I can and will continue to see her the rest of her life. The first time I saw her, she didn't know me and was very incoherent. I couldn't reach her at all.

The house-mother informed me that she doesn't and won't recognize anyone from here on out. If any of you people think she does know you or should become rational—it is strictly our imagination, as my friend is completely out of reality. I didn't believe her.

I went to see her neighbor, the one that kept an eye on her and help her when she started on her walks, as my friend would fall because of a bad hip. The neighbor informed me that for some reason she had completely lost it that night. Was totally out of reasoning and did this from time to time but this time was different. She would just mumble syllables, after quite some time they decided the best thing to do for her was to call in the Police to take over the situation. We had been praying that God would send someone to give her some help as she shouldn't be living alone. Someone with a pure heart and not with greed in their eyes.

"A couple days before this happened", I had been with her most of the day and there was no indication of this sort of thing. I had seen none of this sort of behavior, I would have trouble getting her to understand sometimes because she was getting so deaf. Some of the answers back would be very funny, but we could laugh about them together, once, she understood what you said.

What the neighbor had told me, and how she was, the first time I saw her in the Foster home, was very hard for me to handle, it bothered me greatly, emotionally and spiritually.

I began asking God how can this be, so quickly. I never saw or experienced this side of her. Was it there? and I was seeing with blind eyes? How can they say she has been this way for some time? I would spend many hours at a time with her, she was never incoherent around me. Yes she hallucinated from time to time but she always would come around, with talking and understanding.

I have seen my friend now several times. She is in and out of comprehension (the main thing, its, in and out) We have some, some very rational conversations. There are times she know me by name and other times I can't reach her at all.

The other day while visiting her, in a very clear mind and voice she said to me, "I forgive them; I have to forgive them, God wants me to forgive them for their lying, cheating, stealing from me, for what they have done to me. So I forgive them! I don't care what they do with my things on how much they fight over them, I don't need it any more, I don't want anything more to do with them. I'm free of all those things. They can't hurt me anymore." end of quote.

With that I broke down and wept as that came from her heart and from God. We had studied and talked about possession so many times, and she just couldn't let go—they were so important to her, her life was in those beautiful things and her money, her idols.

I knew then all my teaching and our praying wasn't for naught, God really touched her heart. Now she is free of those possessions that were so valuable in her life, she is free and can go home with peace and knowing she finally did it. That was such a blessing to me to hear her confess that. I knew without any doubt that God would come through. The next day God began to reveal the answers to me as to why I never saw this condition or these things coming about within my friend.

GOD'S ANSWERS

Remember when; the times you would go in and find her crying with torment n her heart—you would talk to her with love and compassion and pray for her peace.

Remember how she would become calm? I would be filling her with inner-peace while you were turning the conversation around and got her talking about and praising me?

Remember: you prayed for her to have inner-joy? and she received. Remember the times she would greet you at the door with a smile and laughter, she would be filled with happiness.

Remember when: you prayed that she could see the word to read along, and to hear and understand? You both were always amazed how well she could see and hear during the Bible lessons?

Remember when: she would have trouble walking because of the pain in her hip? You would pray and agree together for my healing touch, so she could walk, to take her someplace?

Remember when: you wept and prayed for her protection from those that were mistreating her and taking advantage of her? She not always heard and understood the words, but she always received the request and always acknowledged and praised me for her help.

Remember: how excited she would be telling you how she would ask me for help and I'd be right there—showing her where to find something she had misplaced.

She was hungry for my word and you fed her. You stayed with her even when she was full of bitterness and hate. You became weary at times, but you continued on and ask for patience and understanding, The more hungry she became the more your love flowed into her and she opened her heart and became a child into My kingdom

You saw her through My eyes. You looked beyond the surface of what the world sees—you filled her with My love and compassion. You cared, you prayed for her well being, you loved her with My love. You ask and I gave it. You showed her My kingdom and the Glory that lies ahead for her. You taught her well.

That's why you never saw the other side, you saw her with My eyes.

CONCLUSION

Most people I see are elderly terminally-ill. A good 90% are incoherent, and many times I have left wondering if they really hear me or understand anything I say to them.

Even though most cannot comprehend, some seem to feel God's presence—when I give them their hug and tell them how much God love them. Sometimes their face will light up and they will weep. Even though they can't speak what they are feeling, I know that they felt God's touch even though every word may have been lost. What a joy to see them respond ever so slightly.

When Sharen responded with her prayer of Forgiveness to her enemies; that showed me how God can open even the hopeless and lost mind. Nothing is impossible with [unable to read] God, when you want to touch someone.

We should never feel that our efforts are in vain—because we don't know God's mind and power.

You answered my prayers when you showed me that the unreachable can be reached through persistence and faith and prayer.

Every once-in-a-while I have a pity party—I can't do—I'm not good enough—why can't I do things like so-and-so? and on it goes.

But God always comes around and shows me how he uses each one according to our abilities; no matter how awkward or simple or how much I mess up, He's always there to put all my pieces together in their right order and come up with a beautiful finished product.

FINALE

9-29-95

Sharen has not been able to converse or comprehend since her prayer of Forgiveness on Sept. 20th

I went to see Sharen today, again, was asked to leave as I am causing her to become mean and violent.

You talk to her about God and dying and other stuff. She doesn't want to hear about those things. It makes her angry and violently mean, you force her to listen. We can't control her as she hits, bites us and kicks.

She is totally out of control. She is that way every time you come to visit her. Therefore we can't allow you to visit with her. So the family and myself have discussed it and have requested the guardian over her to obtain a medical restraining order from her Dr. forbidding you to visit with her

As I was leaving, the Lord said, "it is finished, there is nothing more you can do for her. Go on to the next. This was of Satan."

I had given Sharen a religious card telling her how much the Lord loves her and how glad I was that she was in the kingdom of God; and yes she was right, they can't hurt her anymore."

Guess that is what set everybody off.

Lord, send me another Sharen.

THE END

The day before this dear lady passed away; God, again gave her a clear healthy mind to witness to a friend of hers that had came to see her.

Sharen told her all about the Lord, and she was standing at the door, ready to open it and walk into Jesus. She was ready, full of Joy, and anxious to go. She was in no pain and felt wonderful; even though she had a very high fever and was very ill with pneumonia. She really loved the Lord and witnessed, just, one more time.

Another miracle of God's mighty hand.

She has gone home now to be with her husband and the Lord. 10-27-95

A PHYSICAL ENCOUNTER

It started one month ago. I see this lady (Veina) on a regular once a week basis. I have been seeing her about two years now.

To begin with she could communicate some, but it was a real struggle for her to get the words out that she really wanted to say. She would always have a smile, a twinkle in her eye and happy to see me. As she knew I wasn't one of those that would make her do something she didn't want to do.

As time went on the Alzheimer's became worse and worse. Every time I tried to talk to her about God she would always say she didn't know what I was saying. But when I would visit her she would have to study me for a while before she would recognize me and let me approach her closer. Once she recognized my face and voice all was well and I could come in closer and talk to her and give her a hug. She would try to talk back to me but scrambled words is all that she could put together. Every time I would tell her how much the Lord loved her I would get a very negative response, as though she really didn't want to hear anything that pertained to God.

The first of this month when I stopped in to see her, she was sitting in her wheelchair in her room.

Week One—
I approached her and began talking to her in the usual manner, and was waiting for her to recognize me before moving in closer to her. She began looking at me with anger and hate and began screaming in an angry fierce tone and told me to go away.

O.K. no big deal as this is normal behavior for late Alzheimers.

So I went out and said I will see you next week; and continued on my rounds.

week2—
Again this time Veina was sitting in her chair in the doorway of her room. I approached her in the usual manner and waited for her response.

This time right off she began screaming and cursing me; but the facial expression was more of a madman.

I turned and politely left and went on my way to the next room.

week 3—
Again she was sitting in her doorway. By this time I wasn't sure what to expect from Veina. So I approached with caution and remained a little farther back than usual. She recognized me right off, and things began to happen.

I was so astonished and engrossed as to what was taking place before my very eyes I was spell bound.

Such anger and hate came upon her face—her body sat up rigid and seemed to puff-up—her eyes became large and jet black and looked like large very dark caves filled with anger and hate—her face slowly changed into demon like features—her mouth began to change shape and she began baring her teeth and began drooling, hissing, snarling, and growling; hideously. She began to speak;

"Let us alone What have we to do with you. Did you come to destroy us?

I know who you are. Go away."

I didn't run, I didn't say anything, I just watched in awe, unbelieving of what I was witnessing. These sounds were coming from deep down in her soul. As I stood and watched the worse they became. Then she began yelling" NO! I hate you, go away." The voice seemed more like a grunting noise but formed into words. She continued to yell those same words to me over again.

I finally turned and walked away in disbelief.

Later in the week there was a sermon on TBN of how Satan is working through his people on the Christians, and gave some examples of such workings which included similar cases of what I experienced.

So I was ready for her the next time it should happen.

week 4—
This time she is in the dining room seated in her wheelchair near a window. As they are gathering the patients for their exercise period. Every patient that is able to be in a wheelchair is brought into these sessions whether they participate or not.

I was making my way around the room; now it is Veina's turn.

As I approached her she began to change into this demon person. I stood close and right in front of her and let her go to almost the growling part; then I stepped up close and looked her right in the eye, pointed my finger in her face and rebuked that demon right then and there.

Again I am astonished and engrossed as to what I am witnessing. This time it is in slow motion and in reverse. Watching that demon unfold and totally leave and go back inside her body.

She became her old self with a happy face and smile and that glitter in her eye but she still refused the hug or any close contact.

I ask the Lord; "Why!" Why did I not rebuke him and cast him out? I knew what to do, as I did extensive studying on that, I knew what was taking place, instead I just stood there like a dumb ninny, speechless, unable to say any thing, just stand and watch it.

answer: I was teaching you. I wanted you to see and understand ALL phases of him. So you will recognize it at any stage and know "you have the power to cast him out".

You will be confronted by Satan's ways many times. I am setting you in his line of fire. You will be bringing the prodigal sons back into My Kingdom. I am sending you out to heal the broken hearted.

Dec 1995

God is teaching me to see people with His eyes. See their inner needs and use my ministry that He has provided me with, to minister to them with HIS love and compassion. To help them through their trial. Lift them up to His glory.

I have been given the wonderful opportunity, yes opportunity to minister to the dying. no this is not a morbid thing of the devil; this is God giving that one who said that firm NO another chance to whisper and call His name "Jesus".; before they walk through that last door.

To be able to read the word, pray and talk "to" them; yes even in their semi-conscious state they can hear and perceive every word you say to them it is such a spiritual time to lift them up before God and help them through their transitional time in their dying process You can read scriptural poetry, scriptures, read to them about Heaven, and hell if need be. Show them what is on the other side of that door that they are preparing to enter through. It can be a very spiritual experience for the both of you. Oh and how God anoints that time with Him.

If this is a child of God you are ministering to it is so much more spiritual. They too seem to enter into this realm, even though they are semi-conscious. Such peace and glory come about them. Lift them up and walk with them to that door. Let that person KNOW you are with them all the way, they don't need to walk that path alone. We all have some fear of being "alone" at that time.

FALLEN: COULDN'T GET UP

A long time friend come across me one day, in a Christian Book Store. She was over-joyed seeing me again, as it has been quite awhile.

In the past I have avoided this person as she is one of those people; when you ask how things are; be ready to listen for two hours of trials and tribulations.

This time was the same old thing, but yet, it was different, somehow. There was a genuine troublesome tone in her voice; something you knew in your heart that wasn't quite right.

We talked, we prayed, she talked, I counseled; but she never received one word. She was too busy talking non-stop, trying to convey her message. Others in the store have also tried to minister to her with no avail. She left after some time with other errands to do. I felt so helpless when she left as I knew I was of no help to her, she left with the same torment she came with.

As she went out the door-it was though something grabbed my spirit and yelled, "go after her—she is in need of help, she is crying out for spiritual help—it is very urgent you minister more to her as quickly as possible, before it is too late."

The clerk at the store got the very same message I had received. So that was confirmation it wasn't my imagination.

When the Holy Spirit speaks and gives you a Firm command, you best obey.

Having not seen her for quite some time I had forgotten her name. Before the week was gone by; between the store and myself, we came up with her whole name, we still didn't have an address or phone number. After some searching I finally got it all together and called her and made a date with her for lunch.

I explained to her the best I could as to why I wanted to meet with her and that I wanted to ask her questions about her personal life; so hopefully I could be of some help to her; emotionally and spiritually. Even though I had no idea how I was going to do this great thing the Lord has ask me to do. She accepted my offer with open arms.

Knowing I was in for a very long spell of non-stop listening; even so, I began asking about her past when things began to go downhill for her. She began with "when my husband died, 20 years ago."

I had ask about her Christian life and church life as it stands today. O.K. Lord you said I had to listen to it all in order to know how to help her and in what areas.

[To my surprise I was able to listen to her with sincerity and patience and understanding. This I was never able to do before more than about ten minutes of it at a time. The Lord already knew it all, but I didn't, so he stepped in and gave me the patience and an open hearing heart.]

All of these trials and tribulations seem to have started about the time her husband died; twenty years ago

After about two hours we left the restaurant and did some errands she needed to do and went on to her apartment; still non-stop talking. After another half hour or so I told her it was time to pray now.

We had to start off by rebuking and binding that old devil to shut off the communications so she could focus on the Lord and not on herself, so all her energy and thought was concentrating on Jesus and His helping her out of this deep depression.

We began by inviting Jesus and the Holy Spirit to come in and take charge, and giving Him Praise and Glory for her deliverance.

As she continued to pour out the hate and bitterness that was planted so deep in her heart, the Holy Spirit began ministering to her through "assurance and promise scriptures". When she could no longer think of any more inner pain we then ask God to fill her cup overflowing with His peace, and Love and inner joy; then I ask her to pour that cupful into her heart; fill up that big empty hole that is now left in there where all that hurt was. At that point we knew she had been delivered of all that stuff Satan put in there, as she began to weep and give God thanks and expressed how that heavy load that she was carrying around all these years are now gone, "I don't feel like I'm carrying a eavy load on my shoulders any more, it feels so light, there is no more weights. I feel so much peace. I give God thanks for His Mercy and Grace." Isn't God Good!

The following week we went through another similar prayer and deliverance time. She still had doubt and hurt; lack of faith; most of all she was still blaming God for all her mishaps and lack of material things that He seems to give every one else and not any for her, He gives it all to those who don't serve Him, why?

We began our payer tie in the same manner as before; then she began to "tell God, out-loud" how she felt about Him and why she distrusted Him, why she felt unloved by Him. Why don't you help me, God?

Then she ask for "Forgiveness and also forgave God.

As she spoke those things to God she began yelling "ouch, ouch", this continued on through out her confessions.

Afterwards she said she was yelling "Ouch", because every time she would tell God why she hated Him she would get very sharp shooting pains, like they were sharp darts, shooting out of her chest and they would hurt, each one of them and they were definitely shooting Out of her. That old devil had to take back all of his lies. Praise God!

The following week we went through the house anointing all the doors and windows and rooms and then anointed Pearl for her protection with the guardian angels from the enemy forces that come against her. And casted out the spirits of depression and suicide.

As we went through the house the bedroom was really strong with the enemy forces. As I began to leave the room the Holy Spirit said to go to the closet. Wow! they had all huddled in there, don't know how they all fit, there were so many.

We then began to cast them out of the closet, As I felt them pass by me, Pearl began to scream "they are on me, they're ahold of me, they are throwing me around." I was beginning to weaken physically then to, as it was draining the energy out of me.

I quickly turned with a burst of energy and cast them off her.

But I was unable to return to the closet and finish the task. I realized there were too many and they were too strong for me to continue on by myself, I needed help. They have such a strong-hold in that place, they have been there so many years and welcomed by past residents, along with reinforcements through out that building. The building has many drug and prostitutes, and witch-craft. The best thing now to do is pray for Pearl to find another place to live. One that has a Christian atmosphere. The living-room was filled with so much peach and tranquility. Neither of us had ever felt that kind of peace so strongly, before.

The following week I noticed the demons had returned with re-enforcements. We would bind them and continue our prayer sessions.

After prayer and giving it over to God and ask His guidance on where to concentrate our efforts, we are now praying and looking for her a different place to live.

Through continuing prayer sessions and studying the word—listening to Christian tapes, Pearl is a whole new person with a new out-look on life. She has that beautiful glow and the glitter in the eyes of the Lord back in her soul. Things are on the up-swing, but it is going to be a real hard struggle fighting off that old serpent, that was pushing her down to his level, now she can hear the Lord's voice once again. He has lost this battle, he is a liar from the pits of hell.

When the Lord told me to help this lady; I said O.K. Lord; but I don't know how, or what, or where, to even begin. It is totally in your hands, I'm willing to do my very best. I can't do a thing in myself, I don't know how and never done this before.

But if this is what you want me to do I'm willing to give it my very best.

When we have to trust in Him totally, things move so beautifully and you see the results immediately before your eyes. God is so awesome. He also can get very firm in his "speaking" through you, to get his word into their heart that He wants them to receive. WOW!

I have been asking the Lord to use me, and He knows I'm a "one on one," kind of person. I never dreamed He would use me in this way. I have been receiving a word and prophesies from different ones from a while now that I would be doing things, even I won't imagine doing. I feel I have skipped three rungs on that ladder. As the Lord has moved me into a whole new spiritual realm. I feel so blessed.

Really—the Lord wants us to put our "Trust and Faith" TOTALLY in Him. That's how He can BEST teach and use us. Lord I pray you will Yell at me and Stop me if at any time, I should begin to get the Big Head or decide that I can do this my way; and that I Follow Your direction only. Let it be Your Will, Lord. Always!

GOD'S "PHONE" NUMBER

Hello God, I called tonight
To talk a little while
I need a friend who'll listen
To my anxiety and trial.
You see, I can't quite make it
Through a day just on my own...
I need your love to guide me,
So I'll never feel alone.

.

AUTHOR UNKNOWN

HE SET ME FREE

After the morning Church service a gentleman inquired of Fred's health as he noticed he wasn't looking and acting his normal self. I agreed; and the conversation ended.

As we left the parking lot of the church the Lord spoke to me and said in His gentle voice; "he will have a Heart Attack at home; it won't happen while he is driving." that all that was said.

A Heart attack hadn't really entered my mind; many other weird thoughts or accidents, but not that one, so—o is God really warning me or is that old devil trying to scare me with these tactics, especially now that someone else drew attention to his health. But because the thought was so gentle and something that hadn't been there before I put it away in the back of my mind. Although Fred has shown symptoms off and on for quite a long time, but he refused to draw it to the attention of his Doctor, refusing to acknowledge that there may be a problem. So I didn't dismiss it, I just wondered, how soon.

About nine pm that same evening Fred started complaining of a pain in his chest on the side. As it didn't subside we discussed it a little and it suddenly got severe with additional symptoms so we agreed it was time to head out. The pain is now down and into the arm. We entered the Hospital about tem pm, Sunday night; with acute Cardiac Thrombosis. (heart attack caused by blood-clot within the heart arteries). They worked with him about half an hour or so then the Doctor came out with that body language and look upon his face that every wife and mother knows without any second thought, of what it means. He just stood in front of me for a few moments and said; "he has a massive heart attack, he has a large blood-clot blocking a main heart artery.

Every thing we have tried hasn't helped so the next thing we need to do is give him a massive shot of Coumadin, which has a very high risk of a stroke but we have no other choice at this point as nothing else is working. We have to try it in order to dissolve and move that blood-clot in a hurry or he isn't going to make it. Even at that it will take at least twenty minutes before we know if it is going to help. If it helps only a little, enough to move it from where it is he will stand a chance. I need your permission; as either way the risk at this point is very critical. If we don't do it he stands about a 98% chance of not coming through; if we try the medicine his chance rises to 50-80% of coming through with some heart damage or stroke.

We have no guarantees now." He left and at this point I called our Pastor. They administered the shot and soon after it became very quiet, no talking, no commotion, no anything. Fred must have went unconscious after they administered the shot.

After a while, what seemed to be forever, the Doctor came out to tell me that the shot was beginning to do it job and he was coming around not but we still don't know how much good the shot will do totally. We are hoping it will dissolve it completely. Finally the Pastor arrived. With a total of two hours Fred was stable enough to move to his room.

When everything became quiet in the E.R., I stood and gazed at the curtain (space) where he lay; I then saw in a vision, two young angels encircled above him about 2 ft., circling around his head and over his chest, they were singing softly to him.

The Doctor was amazed that there was such an immediate and dramatic change take place in him. He continued to improve throughout the night. By the next morning there was such a miraculous improvement they were considering a tread-mill test and adjusting his medication and releasing him to go home the following day if he continued to improve at this same rate. But with continuing chest pains they had foregone the treadmill and moved to walking around instead, and readjusting the medication more.

By morning the physician in charge was so confused as to how, what, and why; he didn't know what to do; all he had to say was; "In all my years of practice I have never seen a heart condition act or react like you have done. I can't help but wonder what you may have done to cause all of this or what went on in the emergency room that may have upset things. As all of their tests and finding are so far off from my testing and findings. I saw at this point you did not have a heart attack; I do not know at this point what you did or did not have—but all of my testing shows otherwise; there is no heart damage or problem at this time. With the severity of what is reported form last night, you wouldn't be up doing what you are doing it just don't work that way with a real heart attack. I don't understand. I do believe you had chest pains, and they are continuing, which indicates looking into, as something is going on. I believe it is all around the heart and not the heart itself. I'm going to call the cardiologist clinic in Portland and talk to them and try to explain what is going on, whatever they say to do that's what I'll go along with, otherwise, I release you to go home, I don't know what else to do with you.

I stand here and I see that not only has he had a miracle physical healing, he has been touched by God's hand. I believe in my heart that he has had a, "near death experience," He has the presence of the Lord all over him, that wonderful glow the Holy Spirit gives you. And he continues to say, over and over and to every one that comes into the room; "He set me Free; He set me Free;" — with such a glow in his face and his body language. Only the touch of God can do that.

The medical personal that was on duty at the time he was in here is stopping by his room and saying; "you are a miracle, most don't make it through the night, nor should you be out walking around the halls this soon, You have a lot of outside help.

The Doctor sent word back that they were sending Fred to Portland by ambulance to St. Vincent for further testing and coronary arteriogram.

We praise and worship God and give Him all the Thanks. He did it all. He had a miracle healing from God Himself.

We know that there are at least five churches that have Fred on their Prayer chains.

When God is in charge anything is possible, especially the impossible

Wednesday morning; Doctors report to Fred that he had a massive Heart attack with total blockage, Sunday night. We don't understand why but all the tests show there is NO heart damage. The Angiogram will be done tonight at four pm. They told Fred he should be dead. They don't know why he came through this and so quickly.

They found a 90% blockage of the coronary artery. At the same time of the arteriogram they did the coronary angioplasty, with a stint. Again they are amazed that there is no heart damage or other circulatory abnormalities. Was released the next day to go come.

Came home Thursday night. The following morning upon arising he felt ill and faint and went into intense chilling. At which time I called the Doctor and they recommended he be brought back into emergency as it sounds that he may have an infection somewhere. Upon arrival he was chilling so intense that they couldn't hold him still enough to give him an I.V. His temp. was 102.2 So again more testing and xOrays. The B.P. was very low and the white count very high and the X-ray indicated he had pneumonia. Again after 24 hours he showed a miraculous recovering. The temp. was dropping rapidly the B.P. and white count too were improving already. The third day he again is released to come home. In spite of weakness and tiredness he is quite well, considering all that he has been through the past seven days. It is now Sunday morning. Heart showed no problems.

It will be a slow recovery back to normal with a lot of ups and downs. We will have sudden mood changes such as; anger, blame, discouragement, depression, and fear, with confusion, forgetfulness.

That's all part of the recovery, the healing process. But God will give us the strength and patience, and walk through it with us

With all the prayers of people interceding, God answered them all. He is he great Physician, the comforter. He held us both in His arms the whole time. Gave us the peace and strength we needed. What a wonderful God we serve.

Again the Door is saying; "You are beating all medical odds, I'm letting you go home." Doctor had told him that he would have to remain hospitalized for seven days. Fred was released to go home the third day.

We could have never imagined in our wildest dreams of having such a large family through the kingdom of God. We knew we had our church family—but hey, the while town turned out; well almost anyway. God showing His power through prayer and faith. Through the family of God.

HE SET ME FREE

part 3—Jehovah-Rapha

God gave us both an inner peace during all the trials and tribulations.

John 15:2
Every branch in me that beareth not fruit he taketh away: and every branch that beareth fruit, he purgeth it, that it may bring forth more fruit.

As we walked through the fire I was totally dependent upon God. I gave it all to Him, all of it. What ever he chose to do we will except without question.

John 15:11
These things I have spoken to you that, My joy may remain in you, and that your joy may be full.

I felt God's presence all the way through. His comforting arms, as He held me, in my weakest times. He was my ever present companion, my rock which I leaned on. Without Him, I don't know how I would have coped. I set and wept for three days just in God's ever presence; praising, worshipping and thanking Him for His healing hand that He had placed upon my husband. He continues to hold our hand, hour by hour. Even now that the immediate crises is past, I still continue to weep with God's grace and joy in my heart.

John 15:7
If you abide in Me, and My words abide in you, you will ask what you desire, and it shall be done for you.

I know God took evil and has made something good from it.

He kept all my prayers for my family coming back into the kingdom of God and will bring back together our relationship in our marriage; that the devil had taken away. He kept all my tears in his bottle, and anointed me as He anoints the earth with rain drops. The vessels were filled, He poured out the old and filled it back with His Love, joy and peace. In God's timing everything is renewed.

John 15:3,4
You are already clean because of the word which I have spoken to you. Abide in me, and I in you. As the branch cannot bear fruit of itself, unless it abided in the vine, neither can you, unless you abide in Me.

It has brought our family together—and now our marriage back into a closeness that was lost for many years. It has brought us much in our walk with God.

And now I ask; Lord would I have; and could I have; spent my time in praising and worshipping and thanking you for your grace and mercy if things had been the other way? IF he hadn't lived?

Here is a toast if you're inclined
to each other to be kind.
Sometimes stop and pretend you are small,
to notice the flowers and trees ever so tall.
Let us be children who never hate,
see in each other God's love so great.
Hear the angels sing thru the birds we see,
hear the trees whisper in the gentle breeze.
With Love, Joy, and Laughter wrapped with zeal,
Remember the past as it leads to the future.

LIFE CHANGE

We later was called in one by one and each was to take a block (styrofoam), take a block for each pain on our list. Stack them up in a corner before God. Giving them all to him one by one. Breaking down our wall.

The next step and last, was to lay down across the arms of fellow members and staff. (Trust, they won't drop up). While laying in their arms they lift us up unto the lord while we listen to music: a song picked just for us. Relax and just listen to the soft music and listen to what God has to say or show us.

While laying there I felt like I was floating higher up into the air. Soon I saw a little girl laying in God's arms being carried as a father would carry his small child off to bed. This was a little girl all dressed in a beautiful white dress with long flowing hair in the wind as they soared off into the clouds softly gently. I looked down into his arms and it was jessie about four years old. We continued to soar higher and higher with the winds. God was looking at me and telling me "I was his little girl". They stood us up on our feet again and had us tell what we had seen or heard. Then they took us over to the full length mirror to see how God now sees us.

At first glance we see our old self. Then we begin to change as God reveals our true selves to us.

I heard him saying "you are wonderful, you are beautiful, you are truly a woman of God, you no longer have to reply, you don't know the real me. Then I saw myself wrapped with his glory.

The next day I heard: you wil be doing the same ministry but you are now equipped for your new ministry. I have taken away and buried all of your old tools and given you shiny new tools.

All 14 of us were in the same movie: we just had different actors: played in different theaters at different times in our lives.

STAND AS THE TREES

While I was walking and talking to God and praising him; he showed me the trees, as I had never seen them as he sees them he said; look, look up into my forest. See the trees which stand tall and stately, gently swaying in my gentle breeze. These trees are as your are, I will show you how you are alike.

* Look up into the tops, the tall straight ones. That is how you are when you are walking in me, and you are mature in your christian walk. The fuller the tops of the trees the more you are in my likeness and serving me. The broken tops are the backsliders. They stumbled and fell, and in their self-pride they didn't think to ask my help, nor cry out to another child of my kingdom for help. No-one came along and helped or prayed to get them back on their feet so they gave up and lived the best they knew how, they only came to my house for special occasions, my birthday and my resurrection, they knew about me but they really didn't know me. Maybe if someone would have come along side and invite them, once in awhile they would come to visit me. They are born again and still in my kingdom.

* The deformed and bent over ones, they too are my children. But as they tried to walk it on their own. But someone saw their brokenness and gave them my hand. They were lifted back up into hope as they were delivered of their sicknesses. They are walking strong and cry my name when they stumble. I guide them down the straight and narrow path. See how straight and up into the light the top goes now?

* Now you see the dead trees with a sadness in your heart. The moss that clings to their broken bows. They are the ones who are dead in their sins. They closed the door and sealed it shut, wouldn't let me into

their hearts. They refused to heed my calling, they said I was someones figment of imagination. My heart breaks for them.

* Now look ahead and see the ones over there, the ones with their green gowns down to the floor. They were dedicated to me while in their mothers womb, and grew with my grace and glory in my fathers house. Those I have set aside to be the shepherds to discipline and lead my sheep.

Then he said look again, look all around, into my beautiful forest; what do you see? What do all these trees have in common?

Yes my child, the dead and broken limbs. Not one was left untouched. Notice how much more some have than others. It took some longer to hear my voice. They tried to do it on their own and failed, before they learned to listen. Believe, trust and obey my words.

This was given to me in a vision at a retreat. March 1996

MIRACLE CRUSADE—PORTLAND
MEMORIAL COLISEUM—SEPT 5, 6 1996

BENNY HINN group 35

Just a note to tell you of my healing at the Portland OR Miracle Crusade. Our group went to all three services. We all were ministered to, and anointed and received some kind of healing. 15 of us.

One received healing of arthritis, Bursitis; one of stuttering;

one delivered of bondages; all, of various physical pains.

I myself was in so much pain I couldn't move, pains just shot through my body, I was sitting and crying from the pain. I had a pinched nerve in my upper back as a result of two compression fractured vertebras from Osteoporosis; and spurs in my lower back from arthritis. Long periods of sitting was torture. The spurs also affected my hips to where it was difficult to walk.

I knew that I would be healed at this crusade but here we are going into the third service and still no sign of anything happening, I was getting a little discouraged but still praying that God's will be done. And I continued to pray for others on the floor that I could see that were so very much worse off than I. Especially the stretcher people, and little baby on the heart and lung machine. I still felt in my heart that I would be healed I didn't how much or when or how, but I knew, I just felt it in my soul.

Service was beginning and I was in so much pain I held back on stand up to participate in the worship as I knew we had a long session ahead of us and I didn't want to get to the point that I couldn't participate even sitting down. You began the prayer during the worship service and the Lord spoke to me and said "I can't do my work if you don't do your part".

So I got up and began to Praise and worship God and somewhere during your prayer the Holy Spirit zapped me really hard from head to toe and threw me back down into my seat. I thought I had broken the seat I fell into it so hard and heavy. The shooting pains were gone and I began to weep uncontrollably. The harder I wept the more the overall pains left. Soon the only pain I had left was the normal backache from tired sore muscles from being tensed up from the initial pain.

Towards the end of the service again during a prayer time our whole group went down. I found out later the everyone of us had a backache from sitting so long and our feet were hurting so bad we could hardly stand on them anymore.

As we left the service and walked to our cars no-one complained about hurts of any kind, not even on our trip home. We had over a hundred mile to go. None of us realized till the next day what all had happened.

I am still pain free. I give God all the praise and glory.

In church the following Sunday, as I stood praising and worshipping I felt my body suddenly begin to totally relax from the top of my shoulders to the bottom of my feet. Then God said "that is how you will feel when I get finished with my work in you"

I can't remember when I was ever totally pain free. I am still pain free I still feel the anointing so strong over me.

We witnessed so many miraculous healings. A gangrene foot turned healthy pink on stage. A lady about 35 was born blind and deaf, her eyes and ears were opened, she could see and hear. People with M.S.

were healed of pain and could walk without difficulty. Cancer, brain tumors were healed, they would disappear – not felt or seen visibly any more. People with seeing and hearing difficulties were healed, didn't need their glasses or hearing aids. People with paralysis got out of their wheelchairs and was walking. Broken bones, crippled limbs were straightened and healed. A four year old little girl had osmosis of the kidney (her kidneys put her urine back into her blood stream,) no cure, was healed, she had no more pain urinating, her color was again normal. A man needing open heart surgery (by-pass surgery) his heart was healed he had no more difficulty breathing and no chest pain. A lady given just two weeks to live from cancer was brought in on a stretcher, she got up walked on to the stage and was slain in the spirit by Gods hand.

As healings were taking place all over the stadium people were falling under the power of God, weeping and being healed.

It was awesome, so moving to see the spirit at work and as it moved around the stadium touching people, anointing them, healing them, delivering them from addictions and bondages.

People walked upon the platform and they fell, under the power of God. No one touching or even saying a word to them. Just the power and presence of Jesus.

Sunday morning the altar call was for everyone to come before God and give Him thanks. As I stood there worshipping and praising The Lord, again the power of God came down on me ever so hard, I could see a flame of fire all around me. As I lay on the floor I could see myself surrounded by a cloud of fire. I thought to myself "people don't stand too close to me as you will catch afire". And the Lord said to me in His sweet gentle voice "It's alright they are supposed to catch the fire".

The full length of my spine was short shooting pains, from top to bottom down each vertebra, one by one. I knew God was still doing a work in my healing, I accepted it as Gods healing and claimed it. I gave Him all the praise and glory. God is so good.

I have been baptized of the fire. I was totally bathed in fire.

Year 2011 – still healed today

SEEK THE BEAUTY

Where has the beauty gone?
Beauty is in the eyes of the beholder
In the memory bank, minds eyes.
Do you see with a childs anxiety.?
Are we there yet? Oh how boring.
Have you seen the beauty yet?
Have you laid on the grass on a starlite night?
Watched the shooting stars,
Wondering where they fall?
Wondered what the dippers are used for in heaven?
Where does the moon go when it hides from view?
Why don't people fall off this planet called world,
Those on the other side or spin off into eternity?
Do you see the beauty yet?
Drive off into the depth of the forest.
What serenity, tall stately trees.
Each in there place and a place for each species.
Look around, careful where you step
Over there johny jump-ups, blue bells, daisy's every direction.
God has decorated the forest floor.
See the beauty everywhere.
Off to the mountains we go, up away like a bird.
Looking down upon the world so high.
A roaring waterfall, cascading down the mountain side.
Flowing through the valley bringing living water
To God's creatures, big and small.
See the deer, long horned sheep browsing on the underbrush.
The birds singing as an angels choir.
Eagles souring high above with wings outspread, so easy aflight.

The distant mountain peaks white with glistening snow.
Do you see the beauty?
Down in the valleys the valley so low.
The green soft meadows, the babbling brook.
A family picnicking while grandpa is fishing.
Over yonder a bee farm. Let's lay on the ground and watch the work.
Quiet now and listen. A buzzing busy hive.
Here come some with their pouches on their legs
Filled with golden stands of pollen to feed the young.
Others with special bags to carry back nector
To transform like magic into honey we like so well.
Over there in the meadow are some deer feeding.

If we could see I'm sure there are many small creatures
Scurrying in the grass. Look beyond, to the rolling hills
How picturesque, such beauty.
Beauty lies all around, see it?
Just some of my minds wondering

A WEDDING INVITATION

I am going shopping today,
Searching for a "special" place.
It must be elegant in all respect,
With reverence and serenity.
No ordinary place will do,
You see, I'm looking for a gown".
I'm to be married soon,
As my bride-groom awaits.
So to the upper-room I go to seek,
For my gown of purest linen,
Must be whiter than snow,
Without spot or wrinkle, you know.
My bride-groom is coming soon,
To whisk me away to a manson,
He has prepared, just for me.
One of great beauty,
Filled with peace and love.
You too, are invited to sup, with me,
At my wedding feast, so grand.

THE VISITING DOCTOR

One night as I lay sleeping I had a dream, or was it a vision? I saw myself lying in bed sleeping and I was very sick, I looked very sick but didn't know what was wrong. I heard someone come into the room and when I opened my eyes there was a figure elegantly dressed in a black business suit coming toward me, and as he sat on the edge of my bed he said; "I have come to see you as I heard you were ill, how are you doing? I was passing by in the neighborhood, I had another patient to see,; I'm your Doctor, remember me?" He had a caring and loving look-upon his face and a gentleness in his voice. I'm wondering, why, did he come to see me, Doctors just don't make house calls on their own free will. I told him I didn't feel sick anywhere and I don't hurt so why am I still in bed sleeping so late and did someone request that you call on me? I feel O.K. I guess I'm just sleeping in. Then he said; "you are very ill and you will even get much worse before you get better, it is all internal, none is external, I will come by again soon to see how you are." And he was gone just as quickly as he arrived, and I immediately fell back to sleep, still not feeling any pain or sickness.

Again I could see myself, I even look much sicker, what is happening? The Doctor said I will get better and he will come back so there is no need to worry about it.

Next thing I knew I was awakened again with the Doctor standing by my bedside and saying; "It is now/Pm and how are you feeling now?" I feel great and ready to get up and get started with the chores of the day I have wasted too much time already, I still don't feel anything. He then replied in his loving voice and a smile upon his face; "you are healed now, completely well, I will go now."

And again he disappeared as quickly as he came.

I have no clue as to what my illness was about coincidence or fantasizing???????

I'm finding that I'm able to do some things that I haven't been able to do since I broke my back. I had to difficulty or pain spading my garden or mowing the grass this spring.

I would say the visiting doctor did some great healing.

Thank you Lord!

THE VOICE OF SATAN

Torment—physical and mental suffering

Heaviness—a spirit of grief or anxiety; oppressiveness; having great weight; a heavy heart

After the situation with my husbands illness of his heart attack and pneumonia; I was hit hard with the spirit of Heaviness & torment

Now all this while, of his illness and healing, I had total peace; except with his attitude of pride and, "I'm doing it my way;" and anger outbursts – to-anyone that tries to be of help in any form. It was just overwhelming me. Out of his mouth would come how good things are and how well he is, there is nothing wrong because my Doctor says so. But his body language was crying loudly otherwise. It was tearing me to bits inside. I didn't dare say or do anything that would be of help with the situation; all I could do is just sit back and watch what he is doing and trying to prove to himself and everyone else; and listen to the empty words coming out of his mouth.

The torment was so bad it felt like something inside me was large ball of short pieces of yarn and I couldn't find any of the ends to start tying them all together to mend the skein, it seemed to just continue get bigger and bigger. And they were flying every which way, faster and faster. All I could do was just cry out to God for help and listen to Christian music, and pray, that seemed to sooth my feelings for a while then it all would come back. I couldn't concentrate on anything; I couldn't read; I couldn't study; I couldn't do any physical work I just paced the floor nervously. I didn't want to talk to anyone and didn't want to be talked to. I could do my volunteer work and be free of the thoughts and feelings, but as soon as it was over everything was back as before.

I kept getting this vivid vision, it seemed to be stronger each time it appeared of my husband receiving a severe debilitating stroke, as his consequence of not obeying what his body was telling him and listening to what we were trying to tell him.

It's been almost four weeks now since his heart attack and another round of pneumonia.

I'm beginning to feel like I am losing my mind. I know I can't keep going this way or I'll be having a nervous breakdown myself if I don't snap out of it, and soon. Well who am I to talk against what my husband is doing for his attitude; when basically I'm doing the same thing; "trying to take care of my problem by myself, my way." I need to go and ask for help. So I came to my senses and went to church and ask to be put on the prayer chain, the both of us. The voice in my head kept telling me: "ask if in My name and it shall be given you." Right away I began to feel the peace and joy returning. I could feel my mind getting straightened around the torment being lifted and replaced with God's Love and Peace.

BUT THEN-------------------

While I was driving, suddenly a black wall would come down in front of me and I would be so distraught as all of a sudden it was like someone was telling me to drive in front of that oncoming car—or you can wait for that big semi truck, that would be more certain and quick death; or you can go on down to the river and drive over the bank, at high tide the water is plenty deep that there is no escape. It's easy, you would be a great help to your husband, he would be so proud of you, especially that you did it all for him.

I assure you, that you wouldn't feel any pain as I would make sure you were killed instantly when you make contact. That would deliver your husband of his sickness and you would be free of the worry. Really that's the only way he is going to get well. You would be doing such a great service. Everyone would be overjoyed of his healing and what you did to make it happen. It's so easy and a very joyous time, you will have instant peace and joy.

Just as quickly; I would hear another message; REBUKE HIM, REBUKE HIM, REBUKE HIM! start praising ME!

After the third time of hearing that message I was then able to SAY IT OUTLOUD. When I started praising and rebuking Satan everything would go away, and I would feel free again until the next attack. This went on for a couple of weeks, every time I was out driving.

The thoughts would come so strong and irresistible and almost in a joyous inviting sounding way. So convincing, so glamorous, sounding. I couldn't believe that I was being confronted in such a dramatic way that I really had to fight this temptation off, with every ounce strength and teaching I could bring up in my being, it all sounded so good and glamorous so tempting.

Finally I went to see a sister and ask for spiritual help. She gave me some scriptures on binding and loosing. I read through them daily for a week or so and once again was freed of the torment, for good.

I thank God for this experience. He allowed me to go through. I can understand more clearly how easy it would be for someone to be so deceived as to go through with suicide. Satan makes it sound so easy and glamorous and how much good it will do for all those involved with your situation; how proud they will be of your sacrifice, that will make everything alright.

THEN I SAW JESUS

The first time was shortly after I received the Baptism of the Holy Spirit in 1993. I had gone forward to the Altar for prayer as my hands were giving me a lot of pain and a problem with using them; I was slain in the spirit ", Falling under the Power of God. While I laid there pinned to the floor unable to move, feeling like I weighed a ton; everything around me faded away, I could hear nothing that was going on around me I was in total peace and serenity, I felt like I was suspended into space, just there with someone holding me up there, it was filled with so much reverence and tranquility, a feeling of never wanting to leave this place wherever I was.

Then a face began to come toward me very slowly, it kept coming closer and closer till there it was right before my face about two feet away. It was Jesus! just His face. I was so overcome with joy and surprise and unbelief that it was really Him. I opened my eyes to look around to see if it would leave, was I dreaming, was it real, was I really seeing what I imagine I was? If it is a dream it will be gone when I open my eyes. YES! It remained there before me, it didn't go away. he then spoke and said, "I am real, I am alive." and He was gone.

He had ear length hair sandy brown in color, midway to His shoulders. Beautiful blue eyes like you were seeing into the depths of deep blue lake. They were loving gentle eyes with so love in them. He had a fair complexion and His face shone with such deep compassion and love with a soft caring smile; beyond description. We have no vocabulary that would describe His Glory.

There was no second guessing, no doubting; you just know when it is Jesus, you just know when you're in His presence.

XXXXXXXXXXXXXXXXXXX

The second time was in the spring of 1996, at a Retreat. The presence of the Lord and the manifestations of the working of the Holy Spirit were so awesome. The power was so strong in the place, people kept falling down under the power, many of us just couldn't remain standing, it was so awesome, it was surely supernatural.

The last time I went down the anointing and the power over me was so overwhelming I felt as though I was being lifted up. Then I remember of suddenly sitting up and I was "transformed" to a garden like presence I was sitting in the middle of a walkway. It was a long trail with flowers on either side and a serene woodsy setting. The path was quite long and fairly wide. I sat all alone, I could hear faint singing in far off and there were many birds singing too.

Then suddenly a wall; like blocks made with clay; appeared at the far end of the path.

Almost instantly a large archway appeared. The scenery was picturesque—the sun shone so brightly.

Every color of green one could imagine. The foreground was a huge green meadow with rolling hills with green trees followed by higher and higher mountains with more green trees, all shapes and sizes. Each with their own shade of green. The flowers surrounding the archway became more abundant and the colors more vivid and radiant. The the longer I looked the more that came into view and the more magnificent the picture became. This truly was God's creation, everything was so perfect. Then a beautiful rainbow appeared and seemed to frame the whole picture.

Then suddenly there appeared a figure of a man—standing in the doorway; tall, strong, well built in average type clothes, nothing unexceptional. He just stood there for a moment as though he too was enjoying the beauty and serenity of the surroundings.

He began to walk slowly, his posture and steps were firm and steady, a feeling of certainty. He continued to walk toward me without any hesitancy. I still could not see his face it seemed to be in a shadow. He came straightway and stopping in front of me and just stood there for a moment and then I was able to see His face as He kneeled down directly in front of me and looked into my eyes. He had such an embracing expression on His face as though He was encompassing me with a caring love and assurance.

His hair was light brown, shoulder length; His eyes were blue as sapphire, His face was peace and loving filled with His Grace; His voice was soft but firm with so much compassion. There was an aura of superiority and reverence about Hi. You could feel the tenderness of His Soul through His hands. They were so perfect and so beautiful.

As He reached out His arms and held my hands in His and looked into my eyes He began to speak these words to me: "My Child I have never left or forsaken you even though at times you thought I had. I have lifted you up before My Father in heaven. It is all gone now, everything has been taken away. Everything is going to be alright, the past things are taken away. Go forth in newness. Everything will be different now. You will not see things the same way. The things in your life are made new. You have a newness of mind. I have washed you with My blood. Now go and minister to the hurting, I will be with you."

He then got up, turned and began to walk away, gradually disappearing as he walked down the path toward the archway. Then He was gone; the beautiful scenery, the beautiful flowers, the wall, the archway—everything—gone.

As I worshipped and praised Him I entered back into reality. I remained sitting a moment while still in the glory. I began gazing to the area of the room in which I saw the arch; there were no doors, no windows, not even any pictures on the wall—nothing –not even any people standing in that area, just emptiness. I remained under the influence of the power throughout the next two days.

XXXXXXXXXXXXXXXXXXXXXXXXXX

BROKEN CURSE

I have known for certain for sometime now that there is a Bondage on me.

As in my ministry I seem to always be cut off—or stopped—like I can't go any further, as I keep running into a solid stone wall, I can't break through or go past it—no matter what I do or how hard I try or how much I pray for it; it's just bang, you can't cross there. It seems to run on forever as far as I can see.

I have been asking for prayer and a break through, and strengthening in my ministry. But it seemed that they just weren't understanding what I was really needing or asking for, as nothing seemed to change.

So I have been earnestly started asking God to reveal to me; or through someone else to me, what this bondage is that is holding me down that I can't seem to get free of.

About three weeks ago the Lord started showing me glimpse of things in my childhood. Things that were said and done in my grade school years of growing up. Things that were very hurtful but I seemed to always put them away that it was never said or meant, that they were just empty words said in anger. It would all go away. But they kept coming back to me from time to time, but each time I would throw them off.

These things began coming back into my memory, things I haven't even thought about or even recalled into memory since those years. The Lord began putting visions into my mind to go along with the words that were said. Each time they were getting more detailed and more vivid, I began remembering other details that had been told to me relating to the visions I was getting. It was like I was putting a picture puzzle together and all of a sudden I was finding all sorts of pieces. The more I ask God the more He would reveal to me. Finally I saw a faceless lady, very pregnant, she was quite young and carefree, she was standing alone; the next picture I received was a large room filled with small children, ages of about two years through six years. They were all just sort of milling around not really doing or going anywhere just supposed to be going. I saw myself stand along the wall at the end of a huge long couch. There weren't any adults to be seen, no toys, just some empty chairs. the next scene I was standing outside in the roadway. It was a beautiful white building with two large white pillars stand on either side of the entrance way. I was quite small about two years old or less, I was very small to the other children, the building seemed like a huge mansion, I felt very alone, but why did I feel so alone, there were all these other children around me, but they too looked sad and lonely. None of them were laughing or playing, just looking at each other.

As I stood and looked around; the grounds were immaculate, beautifully landscaped and manicured. The building really looked stately.

Then I noticed a sign by the road, by the entrance; a huge iron gate. I walked to look at it, I guess I was expecting a picture or something, I don't know what I was really expecting to find as I couldn't read, but I went anyway. All it said was ORPHANAGE.

Well something inside me told me that whatever that was, It made me feel very sad and sick inside. And that it was not a nice place. Then I began to feel sad for all the other children there. There was nothing outside to indicate that there were any children near the building let alone hid away inside. I knew then that this was a place where they put children that were not wanted or loved, they were now out of sight and mind.

The next scene was in a very small house with a very loving lady and a sick man that couldn't walk and had to be in a wheelchair all the time, and that lady was taking care of him and she was taking care of me too, but it was different, because she kept giving me hugs and telling me how much she loved me. It made me feel warm and loved.

Then I realized the pregnant lady I saw had to be my mother, then I began remembering her telling me how she tried to abort me many times but I was to stubborn, so she was stuck with me, she had to give birth to me, and I caused her a lot of pain as I was a very difficult birth and how she hated me and didn't want me from the beginning.

My Father and mother separated when I was about one year old, she claimed him to be worthless: But: when he found out she had put me into an orphanage for adoption, he immediately took charge and took me out of that place and put me into the foster home and filed for full custody for my care and well being.

At the age of six 1/2 my mother came and removed me from the foster home. Why she came and took me, I really don't understand or know, as I was always a thorn in her side as long as I lived with her.

After the Lord revealing all that to me, I realized that time period of my life was my bondage but I still couldn't put a name to it and what it was that I really needed to be freed from.

I still don't know what I have done, except to be born.

Two days later we had a very prophetic lady speaker at our Aglow meeting, call the attention to me of a bondage over me. She ask if I knew it was there and if I knew what it was. I told her yes I knew and I was pretty sure what it was about but didn't really understand what the curse really was. She ask me to tell her what I knew about it; about midway of telling her what the Lord had showed me, she interrupted me, and said, "your mother put a curse on you while you were in her womb, she didn't want you and hated everything you stood for." I see the spirit of REJECTION all over you. I was prayed over and delivered of that bondage.

The anointing was so heavy on me I felt that all my heavy burdensome clothing was taken off of me and I was covered in a wispy flowing shroud; so light in weight I felt as though I had nothing over me and I was floating free. I could feel the gentle breeze surrounding me

Aglow meeting—8-19-97

In asking for prayer, I said: "just what ever the Lord leads, let Him have His way". I was hoping for the deliverance or a word or some sort of confirmation on the issue. Well instead I received confirmation on what the Lord is doing in my life now and why He is moving me into these new areas of learning and receiving from Him at Altar times. Also confirmed why I wasn't to attend the B.H. Crusade in Seattle. He definitely has other plans for me at this time.

Her prophecy was: "The Lord is moving you into a wider ministry field. You will still do some one-on-one but He is moving into working and praying for small groups at first; If I will obey and do as He asks of me. He will use me and I will be doing things I never dreamed possible— but I must obey and do as he ask, even if it seem simple, small, and doesn't feel right. I must do the very next thing He tells me to do. 'It's very important that I do the very next thing He ask of me.'" She repeated this several times.

Also, you are Caleb—yes you are Caleb! Wow the things you will be doing if you will follow and let the Lord lead you.

Caleb had a very strong spirit, he does not waiver, he was a strong leader and obeyed God.

The very next day in my prayer time the Lord ask me to send two encouragement greetings to two different people and showed me what they were to be ministering about.

As I headed to the Christian book store I cut through the dime-store, and as I passed by, the Lord walked me over to the card section there, I thought; they usually don't have anything on the order that I'm looking for but OK I'll look. Well the Lord took me directly to the section and directed my eyes right to the cars I was to get.

As I read them; they said exactly what the Lord had showed me and told me what to pray and send to those people. WOW! almost word for word.

I knew what to look for in cards that the Lord had requested, but finding what he wanted to say, now, that will be a bit more difficult, but OK I don't have anything else to do so I will look diligently to find it. I never dreamed that God already knew where it laid, and it had all the words in it that he is wanting to be said to these two me. Or that he would lead me directly to each card. I didn't have to look around to try to scan them all and hope I would sense the ones, NO God took me directly, note, directly, to them, no scanning no reading titles no guessing or second thought, right to it.

WHAT AN AWESOME GOD WE SERVE!

I knew this was definitely from God; as in my prayer time He not only showed me the two men, but the problem that surrounded them, and He then interceded in praying for their need and began showing me in vision what was going on with them and began telling me what the card was to say, word by word. Only God can do that.

TOUCHED BY GOD

The Lord has been using and teaching me intercessory pray. Then about July it was more and more and putting me into it a full day at a time. It starts off early in the morning about 8 am and builds throughout the day with an anointing and building to a fervent weeping and worshipping. Sometimes I would know who it was for but other times I would not. All the deep cleansing and teaching really began at church camp.

At the Seattle retreat He put me into much deeper intercessory. He takes me out of the world and puts me into the spiritual realm. I have no concept of worldly things around me—just total engulfment with the Lord. I'm now awaiting for Him to take me into a spiritual journey or trip. He has given me spiritual visions but I know that one day He will take me with Him on a trip. Further than one can ever imagine possible.

Again Monday I was in total intercessory, throughout the day and growing stronger by the hour. Late afternoon I went to the phone, thinking I was back to earth for a spell, I dialed Jackie, not knowing why I was calling her in particular, I just did—to my surprise she was home and answered the phone, my mind went blank, what am I going to say, I have to come up with something or she'll think I've lost it, so I ask her about the Luis Palau meeting that's coming up; now I already knew the answer as I was reading it in my hand. OK Lord why am I doing this I have nothing to say to her; but then again the heavy anointing began to fall over me and I knew something was going to happen, then I knew why I called her—I needed her to be a part of whatever was coming about and to encourage and hold me up, and if she puts the phone down that will end whatever is to take place and I will fall under the power; but she hung in there and the anointing magnified extensively.

Then it happened: I heard a loud clap of thunder and just as quickly as it sounded a huge tube like a pillar fell down through the ceiling and totally surrounded me. I tretched out my arms but I couldn't touch either side. I knew at this point that if she left me now that neither of us would receive whatever God has in His plan at this moment.

The power that surrounded me was so strong—I knew that it was God—I felt Him around me. I could see myself standing in the center of this huge tube with molecules of energy were dancing around me, as though they were dancing to music; and there was a light mist floating in and out through the walls of the tube, sometimes they would be in a soft pastel color, mostly pink. While this energy was dancing around and through me—I could see it entering me throughout my body and exiting out through my hands and feet as lightning bolts: (in my mind I'm telling Jackie, don't hang up)—as it was shooting out of my right side into the phone, I could see it travel through the lines and piercing into her body. As the lightning bolts shot out I began intense trembling. As I watched the lightning shooting out of my feet and hands it was colored, red and some were blue bolts. I knew that the reason Jackie was to hold on to the phone while all this was going on in me that God was also anointing her, for some mighty work in and through her.

I saw Jackie the following Tuesday; she said, that she did receive the anointing through the phone and that there was such a moving of God throughout their household all week long the family came together in prayer and worship and reading the Bible and even attitudes and changing of the obedience through the children. There was such an anointing throughout the house. It was like there was a big breakthrough in each and every member in the family. She said she knew that something was happening and going on with me and she could feel the anointing through the phone but never dreamed anything so powerful was taking place. Wow, what an awesome God we serve. God told me that He was going to use me in unusual and mighty ways, but this is unbelievable. I had absolutely no control of what was going on through me.

FREE AND WHOLE

Revival; Holy Ghost AND FIRE! Held at the Christian Life Fellowship church with Pastor Munson, host. The four days were rivers of holy ghost and Fire filled services. Matt 3:11-38:19-11 Chronicles 11:2. All speakers came and spoke on the same verses; only the messages were directed differently by God; all in the aspect of The FIRE. How magnificently God orchestrated the entire seminar.

We not only could see, hear and feel the manifestations of God throughout the entirety of the services. The wind of the Spirit was most awesome, speakers would fall under the anointing power, Some could see, some could hear the roar, some could feel the wind as it flowed throughout the room, especially when you went to the front of the room. Many healings, both spiritual and physical; people were being delivered of bondages, old hurts, curses. Some were being filled with the Holy Ghost And Fire; some were receiving prophesies, some receiving their anointing for their ministries. It was awesome to see God doing all those miracles.

One Session was walking through a line (an arch formed of Prayer warriors). They would touch and pray a word over each person as they walked through, each receiving a blessing and anointing as you struggled through. The power was so strong and overwhelming, most had to crawl through if they could make it on through at all.

After everyone got their composure together they then called together groups for prayer and prophesy. The anointing power was still so strong one didn't stay on your feet long after reaching the prayer warriors. As I stepped forward for prayer and my prophesy—a gentle but strong wind went [POOF]. And down I went. As they prayed over me I began to cry from deep within my soul—no outward tears just weeping from deep within. I could feel my own spirit weeping—a cleansing, healing and emptying out—was taking place. As the cleansing and deliverance went on it would be replaced with emptiness and peace and tranquility.

When I got up I felt so emptied that I would float away at the first breeze. Awesome! Soon after two people of God came to me and confirmed to me that I was set free and MADE WHOLE. Amen.

All the services I attended were of the same or similar manifestations of the presence of God. WOW!

ENEMY NO. I

I was working in the kitchen that day and when I finished what I was doing I stood back to observe what was the next needed task.

Suddenly my vision went wild. It was like I was looking down a narrow tube, highly magnified but sharp and clear; and around the outer part were rings that acted like a magnifying glass but out-of focus due to it's strength. It became stronger as you went to the outer rings. The center remained sharp and clear and you could see far away but yet everything seem to look like it was right in front of you, One could reach out and touch it.

I stood still, not moving my head and began trying different things to see if it were my eyes or is it light refractions from the windows on my glasses. Looking up and down, to each corner and again to the center. It was so strange but I really didn't fear the worst. I removed my glasses and tried all those things again, every thing was normal except the normal blurriness, (without my glasses) but the magnifying effect was gone. It must not be my eyes it must be the lighting on my glasses. I could feel a very strong presence of someone or something standing behind me, but I knew no one was there, every one was busy in other areas of the kitchen.

So I then moved to another section of the room, completely out of the range of the over-head lighting and the effects of the windows sun light reflecting. And tried all the things I had done earlier, every thing was still there. I removed my glasses again, and the strange tunnel was gone. The presence of heaviness was so very strong, the room seemed almost dimly lit, it was so heavy.

So I said under my breath; "Lord this is not of you". Immediately I felt total peace come over me and the Lord said; "Do not fear, I am with you." I then knew this was a trick of the devil. I rebuked him, and it left as suddenly as it had appeared.

The kitchen—Loaves and Fishes; senior lunch program along with the home delivery.

About 90% of the volunteer help is Born again Christians. This all takes place in the basement of a large local church.

There were three new court appointed helpers present there this day— they were not accustomed to this type of fellowship, there seemed to be a loss in communications, at times.

POWER OF PRAYER

Two years ago when I had my eyes examined for new glasses, my Dr. said I had a cataract in each eye-dead center and so far it was only affecting my vision slightly—not to be concerned about it for now; we will see how fast it progresses over the next year or so, if you begin having more trouble seeing, come in and we'll check it again. To my surprise I made it through the two years time without any more trouble in fact I normally don't make it the two years, my eyes begin giving me a lot of trouble after one year. But now I was beginning to have some problem staying with my reading so it was time for a change.

In the meantime I had mentioned my eye problem to a dear sister and prayer warrior, had ask her to pray for my vision, and I did the same. Asking God to spare my eyes.

Now the time has arrived to get my eyes examined for new glasses again. During the exam the Dr does his usual hums, and ohs and aws. Tries out some of his new instruments and gadgets, does a few more clicks and turns of this and that and finally pushes everything back into its rightful place and drawer; leans back in his chair adjusts his spectacles and says; you have a very healthy paid of eyes your vision has changed somewhat in your distance and your reading, but all that is very normal due to your aging; there is no signs of degeneration, diseases, glaucoma, none of the usual, normal or abnormal, problems that go along with aging. I really looked hard to find your cataracts—I can't find them anywhere, I think I can see the faint outline of the sack that they were in, but even that was so faint I'm really not sure that its what I really saw. I would venture to say that you don't have any cataracts either. I know they were there the last time because I have it drawn here in your records, but I just can't seem to find any indication of them this time. They seem to be completely gone. I immediately shouted, halleluiah! Thanked God and rushed home to call my prayer warrior the good news. Isn't God Good!

MY MIRACLE FROM GOD

Returning to the Doctor for a review and more testing in regard to my back problem. He informed me of the seriousness and danger and the possible causes and treatment available—based on the upcoming lab. results. He said the causes look as though there is an easy treatment available to strengthen the bones and to stop the progress now and hopefully to stop any future breakage. As the body isn't absorbing the minerals and that is an indication that something is causing it and I hope to find the culprit.

Well after a week's time the seriousness and dangers and the future outlook all began to soak in. Up to that time I was in total rejection. I didn't want to except what is happening to my bones and body and the seriousness of it all. I tried to pass it off that God is taking care of everything as I gave it all to Him so that settles the whole matter I needn't worry over it.

Well I then went into deep depression and discouragement. I began crying out to God to help me through this time of anguish and depression. After a week in my pity party I began asking God to show me what He wanted me to do now—whoever on however he gives me direction I will receive it. Also during this time I ask the church for prayer to help me through this walk in the valley, that I will have spiritual strength to receive what ever God has out there for me.

Today while working on a word study; God began speaking to me.

First he told me to start praying and he also told me at the same time what to pray for and to, "thank Him," for the miracle he has already performed in me. As the spirit lead I prayed the things God wanted me to ask for. Then He showed me the miracle He has already blessed me with. The fact that I have seven broken vertebras I am still able to "Walk" around and do things with no real trouble and I'm not an invalid and helpless. So thank God for His miracle! Now go and witness this miracle I have done for you and continue to serve me.

My Doctor is not a Christian; he just sits and shakes his head and says; "I don't understand, I don't understand how you are still able to get around like you do, But whatever you are doing it seems to work for you, so all I can say, is continue doing whatever it is that you're doing.

So I share with you my miracle and I will continue to serve God. I have been thanking God every day that he has kept me on my feet and I'm not an invalid and that I have no other broken bones. But this time it was different; different because the thanksgiving came from deep within my heart.

AN AWESOME GOD

MONDAY—This was my day to work at the Food Bank. For our time we are allowed to take a few items home as long as it isn't government issue.

This time I set a couple things aside and began picking and choosing as to what I really needed or could use—than into my little brain, popped; "get things to give to Denny-he needs food. Pick good substantial food as he is sick." OK, there is some good healthy stew, etc. I filled my sack and the whole time I am asking; "God, I haven't seen nor heard of him for a long time. I don't know where he is or even if he is still around here. How would I get these things to him?" I continued to fill the bag; also continuing to question what and why. I must be seeing him soon or I wouldn't be doing this.

FRIDAY—I go to the Star of the Sea rummage sale with a friend, Jackie; It's Free day so I'm looking for text books and reference books I can take to the Juvenile Correction Center as they are in great need of such items. After we finished there, we stopped, and had a cup of coffee to rest and get some visit time as we haven't seen or spoke with each other for quite some time.

She began telling me how God spoke to her about Denny while she and her younger son were shopping for Father's Day. "God told her to go back and buy a pair of jeans and a shirt that was on sale, for Denny and give them to him for Father's Day." There was only one of each, of his size left. So she did so, as she was instructed. Puzzled she ask, "God why? I haven't seen or heard from him over a year, I don't know where he is or if he is still in the area. How am I going to get these to him?"

As she approached the bridge on her way home—there was Denny walking home from the store, where he had bought some bread and milk. This is about four miles from home. She stopped and invited him to ride home with her and she would drop him off to his home. Well he is going her way, he lives in his boat house (scow) on Youngs River. She was all excited as to how every thing is working out. She gave him his gift and he told her that he has been very sick for quite awhile. She then looked him straight in the face, and didn't recognize him.

He was so thin, just skin and bones; really looked bad, very sickly. The ride was short so there wasn't much more conversation except he said he wasn't driving. (he has a history of DUI's)

When she let him off at his place and as he walked toward the houseboat; God showed her that He has placed Denny where he is as He is going to use him on the river with his boat. Didn't show her how or why—just that he had everything in order and he was staying there for a reason. God is purging and humbling Denny that he may cry out unto God in repentance. That he might be used of God in a mighty way. She took me home and after she left, I remembered, I had that food bag put away high in the cupboard for Denny, and this was the time. So I called Jackie back and ask her to come pick up the bag of food I had here for Denny. Then I told her of my tale. Wow! How God works. I told her Denny would be calling her back shortly. She said she didn't know if or when she would be seeing him again, if ever, as he didn't come to visit them any more and he isn't driving so he isn't getting around like he'd like to.

FRIDAY NIGHT—Denny called and came by Jackie's with a friend, as he has a mower there for sale, which was perfect timing to give him the food.

God worked all this out—every little detail, the timing of each person involved; in His miraculous ways. What an Awesome God we serve! How God spoke and used both of us separately, but yet together, in unity; neither of us knowing anything going on with the other. We had no conversations or thoughts about Denny over a long period of time.

We even hadn't visited with each other for quite a long time to know what was going on in our lives, as we are both busy doing our own thing.

God saw a need; called upon His servants; and brought it all together in His timing.

It would have been impossible for either of us to have done this deed in ourselves.

ANOINTING

It all started in church service—it just keeps pouring down over me in waves. I weep for no reason as it continues to flow over me.

7-21—Aglow picnic

Lorna read my testimony of my miracle healing of my back at camp: as she read it, the anointing again began to build gradually. But I tried to keep it under control. The president of our group ask me to come up and lay-hands on the members with back problems for their receiving greater faith that God will heal them also. I wouldn't have to say anything, there, others will do the praying, just move down the line and lay-hands on each one. O.K. that sounds easy enough although I don't feel anything great going on in me. But the same time I'm saying; I really don't want to do this, I don't have the gift of healing. But I went anyway telling God; this all up to Him I can't do any of this stuff. I don't feel very spiritual.

As I laid hands-on and began praying I felt like energy was pouring out of me and through me; God is truly doing something big here. As the power grew, I told Lorna she was on her own; I'm going down. The power continued to flow through me in a tremendous way while I lay on the ground. The girls praying said, they could feel the power flowing from me through them. The girls receiving the prayer said, they too could feel the power flowing through them.

I have heard of a case where God has used a person as the power source while others did the praying for people. Is this what God is preparing me for; to be used in our church body in this manner?

Well, its O.K. Lord if this is your will for my part in the body of Christ in our congregation.

While going on my rounds at the care center the anointing again would very strong with certain patients. I would pray for them; I know they too could feel the presence of the Lord. In fact one lady I have been seeing for five years and witnessing to was very serious this day. I again began witnessing to her like I have been doing in the past. This time to my surprise she was open. Just freely opened up to hear me and ask some questions. One of which was how can I do that? I ask her if she wanted to ask Jesus into her life? She said; yes. I then ask her the usual questions before leading her into the sinners prayer and ask her again if this is what she really wanted to do? I thought she might be saying this to shut me up and get this subject settled once and for all. And again she said yes. There was no mockery, blasphemy, no smart remarks; or I'll have to think about it; or yeah I know someday maybe. We have our little talks all the time, God and me, I talk, he listens, to my troubles. And on and on her comments would go I always answered her as to which God are you talking to?

She said the sinners prayer and I prayed for her pain and wellness. She was very receptive of the prayer and seem very relieved and seemed to have a peace about her that she has never portrayed before. Persistence does pay off. Praise God. I never gave up, just backed off and played it cool and slow; but never totally putting the subject away. I kept bringing it up now and then; each time reminding her that her time was running out, and I'd again tell her what hell was like, and she had a choice to make; that we don't know from minute to minute what lies ahead for us; life or death.

Praise God. I expect to see a changed attitude.

8-1-98 The anointing continues to flow, it comes in waves, sometimes. I don't even have to be thinking about God, it just comes on me. I have also noticed that during praise and worship times my hands and arms begin to tingle. Starts at my finger tips and flows down and up my arms intensely to my elbows. It is stronger in my right hand than my left.

Also when we extend our hands to someone being prayed for it again comes in. When I quite asking God for specific gifts that I wanted and said "Lord you know my desires but let it be your will that I might be a better servant to You" that is when things really began to change in my life.

7-30 I see the lady once a week. Yes she is still a very sick person but the attitude was totally different. She was sitting in her wheelchair reading and laughing, not being negative about everything around her and her illness.

SPIRITUAL EYES

I had finished my prayer time and was starting to leave, when a voice said; "ask for Spiritual Vision".

So I said; "Lord Jesus I ask for Spiritual vision to see, as you see things, in the name of Jesus." I didn't ask for any specific thing or time.

"Immediately, I saw my friend standing before me. Wow! (Vision)

He was sixteen years of age, had a pet snake. Both he and the snake grew to full adult size before my eyes in seconds; but he still remained the age of sixteen. But in the adult size the snake was a massive Boa-constrictor; draped around his neck and down over his shoulders in front of him to the floor. As I looked down its head and tail lay on the floor. The face of the snake appeared to be smiling. The tip of its tail was twitching; like a cat twitches its tail before striking upon its prey. Then the voice said "this is the spirit of untruth."

The snake began as a fascinating toy. It soon became his pet and companion. But as it grew and matured his fascination soon turned to boredom. He continues to try to pull it off and get rid of it, but he cannot free it from his body. It now has become a part of him and it has became such a heavy burden he can barely stand and hold its weight any longer. His face is saying, "I don't know what to do to rid this thing off of me. Please help me to be free of it."

Then my spirit began deep weeping as though I was going to burst with grief. Then I could see and feel a hand enter into my chest and take out a part of my heart. I could actually feel it being taken out. I also felt relief and peace after that.

All the vision left me at that moment.

Gods answer;—

Romans 6:5-7 (NIV) Dec.

If we have been united with him like this in his death, we will certainly also be united with him in his resurrection.

For we know that our old self was crucified with him so that the body of sin might be done away with, that we should no longer be slaves to sin.

Because anyone who has died has been freed from sin.

Romans 6:3,4 (NIV) Nov.

Or don't you know that all of us who were baptized into Christ Jesus were baptized into His death?

We were therefore buried with Him through baptism into death in order that just as Christ was raised from the dead through the glory of the Father, we too may live a new life.

(Then I heard God say loud and clear: "If your friend will obey my command and be baptized in water, I will then deliver him of the curse that is upon him".

8-14-99

After I returned from WOP Retreat—

As I sat in my chair at home—as my husband stood before me talking—God showed my husband to me in the spirit. He was clean and a beautiful person. His confusion in his mindful thinking is his illness, not how he really believes. His heart is pure. That is the deceiving of the devil putting those thoughts into his mind.

His heart is pure that is not of him but of the devil.

Thank you Jesus. God is warning me of more to come and to look to Him for strength. Pray not criticize him.

VISION FROM GOD FOR THE
WOMEN OF GOD

I was awakened with what I thought was a terrible nightmare. Tried to walk it off—but each tie when I returned to bed the vision returned more intense than before. After the third and fourth time. I realized this was not a nightmare, God is trying to tell me something. So I said, "OK God, I get the picture. I'm sorry I'm so slow, I now realize you are trying to tell me something of importance."

God then answered and said, "OK, NOW:

The Vision—The Intruder

I was standing in a very large room; empty; nothing in the room; no windows, no furniture, not even any doors: EMPTY. Then suddenly a very large Blanket appeared in the center of the room, laid out flat, not even a tiny wrinkle in it, plain, no pattern, except for a narrow blue stripe all around the outer edge. There were four people, one on each corner. They were women kneeling and praying in silence. One was myself and three others [Hope, Coleen, Shawn].

One woman was a poor black Slave; looked down upon, of a very young age; One was an Indian Chief's wife with Authority, middle aged; One was a rich lady in all her finery and of high Status and elegance. The other lady was a common, average, every day person and was very elderly Nationality and age seemed to be of no importance.

Suddenly there appeared a large burly, macho man, standing in the center of the blanket. He had, like war-paint, on his upper body and face. He was holding a very large basket in his hands. It looked like it was full of children's toys—I could see baby rattles, dolls of different sorts, sticks and—bones??? along with other items I could not identify sticking out and over the top of the basket. He then set the basket down on the floor and began sorting through the items as though he was looking for, just the right one. He then took an article and came to each one of us individually; shaking the item vigorously and chanting and dancing intensely; over and around each one of us. Each item seem to have a specific formula. He continued this with each item and each person until he finished with all the items in his treasury. But the four of us stood firm, and continued our praying, unbroken, but any or all of his ceremonies.

After exhausting all of his spells he again stood in the center of the room by his bag of tricks and looked around at each one of us and said "I see I have made no impression or able to break you down with my magic spells, they had no effect on you; you were stronger than I; But—I have one more trick up my sleeve that I know without a doubt this one will surely crush you, then you will see my power. He then began digging down deep into the basket and pulled out two strange looking bottles of liquids and a large wooden bowl. He then poured some of the liquid from each one, into the bowl; reached into his pocket and threw in some powder stuff and began to mix and kneed the mixture. He continued to mix until it became a white liquid paste substance. "Now, I am ready for you." Again he began his chanting and dancing, more vigorous than before, and started around the circle of us. About in the middle of his ceremony he would pick up some of the paste from in the bowl and throw it hard onto our back and dart at us as though he was beating us. He continued around the room doing this vocalized encounter. As I stood and watched, one by one we fell into a heap and began weeping in sorrowful repentance to God.

Three of us fell; but one; the slave girl; remained on her hands and knees and continued praising and thanking God.

The Witch-doctor then vanished; as mysteriously as he had appeared.

We then began weeping in shame and repentance and asking God Why?—Why did we Fall? We all thought we were strong enough to withstand against anything the enemy would come against us with. We were strong in our Faith and in our trust in you, God.

God's answer was; "The pressure become so great; beyond your endurance; Your faith weakened when you took your eyes off of Me and onto yourself, even for just that second; that was just enough time that gave the enemy the hold he needed. Because the time is so near of My Coming the Enemy has to pull out every trick he can, to win back, his followers. He will try every means known to break My people. Some will fall, and stay fallen; as they won't have the Faith strong enough to get back up or there won't be anyone to reach out and help them back onto solid rock. You must keep your eyes on Me at all times, keep in prayer and feed upon My Word. It doesn't matter what nationality or where you stand on the Social ladder.

I'm coming soon, so very soon!

(I saw the peoples faces in the natural; the bodies were changed into different cultures and appearances.

I was wide awake the fourth time He showed me the vision.)

The blanket was pure white with a single narrow blue stripe about six inches from the edge with a white tassel containing a single woven blue thread attached at each corner.

The room felt like we were in the Holy of Holies, everything was so pure.

MIRACLE HEALING

At the time of a yearly physical the Dr. found some lumps within my bladder and that they were very painful along with localized pain and shooting pains over a fairly long period of time. In fact with the examination the pain was excruciating and lasted for three weeks after the exam. My Dr. then ordered some further testing within the bladder with an urologist to determine the origin of the lumps. Past records show crystal formations and stone formations within the bladder walls that had been removed; and was fearing a similar problem has again occurred.

Things kept coming up and the testing was prolonged until mid January, two months later.

Being very concerned and knowing that this problem could be much more serious, like cysts or tumors; as there had been growths in the past; I called our church prayer line and ask for healing prayer right away. After one months time all the pain and shooting pains have subsided. I immediately began claiming the healing and praising and giving thanks to God for it. Claimed it every day.

Finally the day of the big examination arrives, mid-way through, the examining Dr ask what and why did my Dr order this testing?

He said: I find nothing! The bladder walls are clean—no crystals-tumors-nothing- a very normal healthy bladder. The color, texture and veins, all look perfect. I give you a clean bill of health.

I still have no further pains and continue to give God all the Glory.

DISAPPEARING STRANGER

While hurriedly walking back to my car, in astoria; I was confronted by a gentleman for some small change for a sandwich. The first thoughts are boy that's a new one. I slowed down momentarily and thought, oh well, but I remembered all I had was a little change and that was at the bottom of my purse and I didn't want him to think I had to search through all that junk in my purse just for a few cents so I kept going, but as I got half way into the intersection I turned around and went back and was going to dig out what little I had. He was sitting about ten feet from the curb so I knew he would still be there waiting. He was sitting beside the open door of the dress shop, leaned up against the pillar. Sitting on a three legged milk stool. But when I got back he was gone. I hurried and I knew he couldn't have totally disappeared that quickly. I ask the lady standing in the doorway if she had see where that gentleman had gone. She said what man! The one that was sitting right there by your door. Lady I have been standing here the whole time and there has never been any man sitting or stand here by me, I think you are mistaken. Ooooooh my! I continued to search all the close surrounding stores knowing there weren't any that a man would be patronizing and there were no food vendors close. I went clear around the block, determined to find him now. So I began to retrace everything in my mind. This man was very well dressed, clean and neat, why would he be pan-handling? Oh dear, that must have been an angel in disguise, and I blew it big time. It's now about 4 pm and I knew most all the church doors are closed for the day and I didn't want to go to the catholic church I just didn't feel right there. So I headed up the hill to the first christian church, that's where I was baptised and was married I would feel ok there. Sure enough the pastor was there and let me in. I told him my wild story and ask if O could go to his altar and pray, I felt I need to repent for my stupidness. When I came out the pastor said, "it is strange that you should come along at this moment as I am preparing my sunday message on the very thing you just told me, helping a stranger." When I got home, in the mail, was a letter from the feed the children, I guess you know I sat right down and wrote out a check.

A SONNET OF LOVE

God made man and declared it not good to be alone,
He then made woman to be a help mate for man.
He made marriage an ennobling influence
of development of a complete life.
He constituted marriage as a union
between one man and one woman.
the growth of affection between Husband
and wife shall grow as the years pass.

When the wind blows fierce and the thunder claps,
and lightning darts hither and thither,
fear not for its light-year is nigh.
Wait for behind every cloud there is light,
As the rainbow glows with her shining array
to fill your days in all his glory.

The Noble Lion is the king of beasts
his roar is loud and steadfast.
With all his brutal strength he shares
his tenderness with great finesse.
His mate respects with no reproach
still she nurtures with devotion and tenderness.,
as their Love is first-rate.
Your affections will entwine
as you grow and bend as the mighty Oak.

MY DIVINE APPOINTMENT

I'm getting information about the Benny Hinn Miracle Crusade, for Memorial Coliseum in Portland. Well, should I put together a group again for this one? I'll wait and see, if its Gods will; people will begin calling me about it. Lords it's all up to you.

About two weeks after the information starting coming in the mails locally, the calls started. O.K. that's the clue. Six weeks to get this together. I started with motel reservations. If that goes right through; That is confirmation it's a go! sure enough; reasonably priced and within two miles from the Coliseum. Last time I tried this, even though God said no; and the doors closed, on every which way I turned. Everything I tried, I fell flat on my face. Some of the people got very angry with me for stopping, not trying harder. Well when God says no, He means no. I had to learn that lesson the hard way as many other lessons I've learned that way.

Things were coming together faster than I could keep up with, people calling; arrangements to make for this and that. Faster and faster things seemed to be coming my way. When it all came time to go we had a total of 27 in our group. Each time we'd call to see if we could get more rooms, it was there, just as if God had His hand on that door and holding it open for us to fill it.

Here we are seated in the Coliseum way at the far end, could barely see the platform. That's O.K. God is everywhere. We have come to praise and worship, to give and to receive what ever He has in store for us.

A week prior to this day, the Lord told me I had "a Divine appointment". O.K. is this really God speaking or my selfish thinking.

But on one of the Christian T.V. programs; one of the sermons I was listening to; the speaker stopped for a moment and said "I have a Divine appointment", and carried on in His sermon. As though it was all part of it. My Spirit almost jumped right out of me when I heard that and I knew right then that was my confirmation. It wasn't all in my head after all it really was from God. We had been sitting for about four hours before the service really got under way. I was really in a lot of pain by now, couldn't find any position, standing or sitting to relieve it; so I said; "God, help me with this pain, we still have a long way to go in this service, I don't think I can handle this four more hours." I then stood up and joined in the singing. Suddenly the power of God hit me and threw me back into my seat. I sat there for a few moments and then I began weeping uncontrollably. I knew I couldn't stay there I had to stand back up and continue with the praising and worshipping. Soon as I raised my arms to enter in, the Holy Spirit hit me again very intensely, and I began shaking violently and the Lord said; "move around." So I began moving my shoulders a little, still not quite sure if this was for real. Again the Lord said; "Move, move things that hurt." So I carefully began moving areas that I couldn't do without a lot of shooting pain, nothing happened, and the pain I had, was gone. The more I moved the stronger the power became on me, I felt like something was squeezing me tightly, but so gently, from head to toe, I knew God was healing my back. I began thanking and praising God. That's all I could do from then on, just thank Him. Because I hadn't came out of a wheel chair with my back problem the people on the floor weren't too sure that I had really been healed, but we convinced them this was for real.

They sent us to stand in a line and there were people standing along the side the whole length. Some praying, some asking questions and some Drs doing simple testing. They were shoulder to shoulder the full length; 2 or 3 praying, two asking questions, 2 or 3 more praying then a Dr asking questions and commanding you do simple tasks—one that you shouldn't be able to do if you were not healed. If you passed that post you were sent on to the next set. And so-on, I fyou failed the test you were sent back to your seat. Many were being sent back. We made it all the way through, now at the base of the steps leading up to the platform you had one more final test from another Doctor. All along the way they kept asking where my wheelchair was. I told each one that God has allowed me to continue to walk on my own to be a witness for the people I see every week with similar back conditions. Yes, I would tell my people of my back condition and how God was helping me walk and endure the pain and admit to them that there were bad days and good days, and of course they couldn't believe. The last and final test before they (dragged me up the stairs); a Dr. ask me to put my two hands together in front of me and extend them as far as possible, then he said, "I will place my two hands on yours and push down and I want you to lift mine up as far as you can;" he did; I did, then he said "yes, she is healed."

I could not even peel potatoes, I couldn't stand the shooting pain from just the weight of my own arms, in my back. The last two and a half months I had injured my spine again lower down and was having much difficulty walking and by evening I could barely get around; I feared there were more fractures.

Before we left the motel room to go to the Coliseum, I took off my brace and said; "I don't need that any more and threw it on the bed." I stopped and wondered why I said, "I don't need it any more, with such assurance". I had seven fractured vertebras in my upper spine that we knew from x-rays and suspected two others. I wore the brace most of the past six years. Prior to that I had a full body brace I wore most of 40 years for curvature of the spine. Seven years ago I was healed of that at church camp. I then went into the fracturing business and back into another brace. I am now free and healed. NO PAIN! I didn't realize that I had been in constant pain until now; that I'm free of pain. As a bonus I was also healed of Carpal Tunnel Syndrome, which gave me a lot of trouble and pain while driving and sleeping That too is gone.

Don't we serve a great God? I thank God, I give HIM ALL praise and Glory. thank you Jesus!

After they helped us down from the platform, they sat us in some chairs and we were ask a lot of question and had some papers and releases to sign. To get a Dr's written report of our medical record concerning our condition, a written testimony from us and our physician. And a release form to be put on public television.

I am able to turn and twist from the waist, roll my shoulders, and stand straight. All things I could not do before.

This was our fourth Crusade of Benny Hinn.

TALKING ROCKS

As I sat at the rivers edge and prayed—suddenly the water before me was no longer quiet and calm; it began forming long rolling waves as though a big ship had passed by and now the wake was coming along; only there was no ship nor row-boat anywhere to be seen, in any direction. It was happening only right in front of me, everywhere else the water was still and calm. The waves were not coming on an angle as a wake would but straight on, toward me. They became bigger and bigger and louder and louder, soon it sounded like an angry (warlike) waves at the seashore after a storm. They began about a foot high and crested like large waves do at the beach, the louder and faster I prayed the faster and louder and bigger the waves became.

Then suddenly I stopped praying and the Lord said; "I am taking away and washing and cleansing—where do you want me to use it?" I then stood up and stretched up my arms out and over the water and ask; God to quiet the tormented waters of our souls and wash us and fill us with his peace and love; wash and cleanse this, area, the heavy dark cloud that hangs over us. Soften our hearts that they will receive you and serve you to the fullest."

As I stood and watched, the waves began to settle back down, and the water again became still and quiet. As it was before.

The waves were grabbing and tumbling the rocks at the waters edge as though they were being washed and cleaned. They were rolling and tumbling as though they were crying out. Some were being carried back into the water to stay. The rejection of the Lord. While others were gently tumbled and moved to higher ground.

The size of the area affected by this wonder was about a 75 foot square area. All around, outside that area the water was perfectly still and quiet

HERE I COME, READY OR NOT

10-15-99—strong thoughts come to mind today that it is time to seriously look for another car. this one is having, to often and to many needs and there are things unattended to due to lack of funds. Besides the mice have the wiring half eaten. I think it's shorting out somewhere.

10-18-99

Going home from town, I pop in a praise and worship tape and God led me into prayer for a very ill friend and sister. So merrily on my way listening to the music and talking to God; suddenly! a car turned right in front of me—not one car-length away. (mind flash—suside! No! I won't help you) I slammed on the brakes and tried to turn to the rear of his car. The brakes pulsed three times and then grabbed. Due to the stormy weather I just continued sliding right for that car. (mind flash-look out here I come, ready or not) Now surely God must have a sense of humor to put that kind of words into my mouth at such a terrifying moment when one is about to wreck their car.

I had hoped to hit him in the back end of his car but instead I hit him broadside with my right front, spun him around as the pavement was very wet. Even though I was only traveling about 25-30 at that time as I hadn't gotten up to speed yet from a previous stop. We both thank God that he didn't have any passenger as they would have been hurt seriously as the passenger side of the car was crushed way into the car interior.

After the gentleman left to call the police I then suddenly began to hurt severely in my lower back, I couldn't move from my waist down. I then became frightened and (mind flash—ambulance and hospital bed) no way, there is no time for this sort of thing)

OK God this is in your hands I need your help. I have no time to be laying around in bed—there is too much to do yet. I can't do your work when I'm laid up. Even though I have lost my wheels I can still manage to get around and go. Beside those people wouldn't understand whey I'm not coming to see them. So please put your healing hand on the pain area and I ask you to heal it. I declare it done and I thank you.

At that moment the car filled with Gods presence, I could feel angels in the back and there was a man sitting in the passenger seat, I could see him, he was dressed in a nice black suit and Peace, Love, and Compassion was emitting from him and into me. I have never felt such total peace and calm in such magnitude; all fear, anxiety, and all pain left immediately. I just sat and thanked God, over and over, again and again.

Now the young man has returned from calling the police and ask to sit in my car with me while we waited for the police to arrive as he couldn't close his windows, they were gone. My passenger was stuck we couldn't open it so he sat in the back seat. We both commented about the good job our seat belts did holding us fast to our seats. (mind flash—don't talk to him or look at him, wait for him to speak first) So we both sat and watched the traffic zoom by us and watched for the police to arrive. After a few minutes he said; It was my fault, you couldn't have missed me no matter what you did,

HERE I COME

I thought I could make it, so don't blame yourself."

A few seconds then the police arrived and right off the young man spoke up to the officer and admitted the whole thing to him. The young man was still quite shaken but I could feel him beginning to relax and calming down. [how could he do anything else with a car full of God.]

After all was completed and we each went on our way. Yes we were able to drive our cars home then, but now they set all crumpled. later that day when I went out to remove my belongings from the car as it is now not drivable, something with the steering is bad. While picking things up as they were scattered around the car, I find the Bible that I keep in the car was resting in the seat where the man was sitting. Then I find my church Bible on the floor under his feet. I had forgotten to take the Bible out from church, I normally don't leave it in the car. Poor man he was surrounded on all sides by God, he didn't stand a chance. I even have a sticker on my dash that reads "Wherever you are God is" that was right in his line of vision.

While talking with the police and the young man; I was so calm, cool, and collected; oh yes and polite, (sickening so) I couldn't believe what was coming out of my mouth—God this surely must be you it surely isn't me.

So I see, God was in full control from the very beginning. Somehow I feel totally different. Can't explain it, cept I feel like I'm totally surrounded by angels. I guess through this God is doing something spiritual within me. Isn't God Good!

Except for my pride broken I'm fine no broken bones; other than that I feel like I was rolled down a mountain side in a barrel. Every muscle in my body is sore.

THE MAGIC TEN DOLLAR BILL

Leaving fred meyers, heading home: I was tired, it was just another cloudy dismal day, I just wanted to get home and rest.

As I sat waiting for the light to change I noticed a family of three standing just off to the side of the street bundled up in heavy coats and looking tired and weary. They were holding a sign up that read, "out of work, car broke down and no money, we are hungry."

Well there is a lot of people that work the system with that hard luck story. I just don't know to believe them or not, besides all I have left for the week is ten dollars.

The light changed to green and as I began to pull out a voice said give them the money. With no where to stop and park I quickly circled the block. As I was driving back to where they were I was wondering if they would still be there or was this another testing.

Sure enough they were still there so I stopped and gave them the ten dollars and blessed them an said go to McDonalds and get something to eat.

I know that ten dollars would get them more than enough to get filled up on there. There were three of them a couple and a girl about ten yrs old. The next day when I opened my change purse to get out some change there was ten dollars in there. I knew I really gave them that ten so how did this ten get in here. I surely didn't have it nor put another one in there and I didn't ask my husband for more money. I know without a doubt that I handed them the ten dollar bill. God is so good.

LOVE, JOY, FAITH

Christmas is a time for sharing,
a time to give; one-to-another.
Time to share our Love, Joy, and Faith,
whether it be a word or a gratuity.
A token of Love, only comes from with-in,
family, friend or foe—it matter not.

Christmas is a time for Joy.
The Joy we shared in times gone by;
so shall we have in future perfect.
As you give Joy, one-to-another,
you shall receive ten-fold....untold.
Though it may be a helping hand or bent ear.

Christmas is a time for Faith.
The Faith we share with one-to-another,
for the things past and the things un-for-seen.
For Faith comes from our conception or mental creations,
we can work with it for good,
or toss it aside and have emptiness.

Love, Joy, Faith.
We are nothing with-out it.
Christmas is a time to Thank God;
for the birth of his son Jesus.
For all these things are impossible
without Love, Joy, Faith with-in HIM.

Amen

REVIVAL

A wonderful two weeks of revival meetings –many new converts every night. With many physical, emotional and Spiritual healing. A new heart, broken bones healed, physical illinesses, Hepatitus, ulcers, depression etc. many more that were unmentioned. Demons were cast out, generation curses broken, bondages lifted.

A breakthrough of the heaviness and darkness that lies over our area. A Buddhist statue (a God) along with many pagan gods were removed from a local motel lobby and artifacts removed throughout the complex. The manager and several of the staff were converted to our Lord and savior Jesus Christ.

Manifestations of many of the gifts were seen and heard along with signs and wonders. Gold teeth, gold dust on a bible, gold flakes on a face. Oil drenched hair, beads of oil appearing in hands. White feathers floating around and on people. Many people falling under the power of God and laid on the floor for long periods of time throughout the building. A breakout of Holy laughter, weeping uncontrollably. All through the influence of the Holy spirit moving in and around the congregation.

I was healed of bursitis in my left shoulder. I realized it was totally gone the next evening service and never to return again. The fourth night I was delivered of "Fear of man". I felt it leave as though it was a stomach sickness. I felt freedom. During the fire walk in the tunnel—someone fell on me and my ankle and foot was injured. I ask for prayer in the following service, as the pain was in my entire leg and foot. Shortly after the pain disappeared. The next night the swelling and redness was greatly subsided, and was mostly gone by the following day except for the discoloring in my foot and ankle from the injury. I know God did a lot of other healing too.

The following service three people mentioned to me how happy they were to see my husband go through the fire walk, and that he had come to the revival meeting. I convinced them that he was not in attendance that he does not attend these meetings. The pastor too said she had talked to him and welcomed him. I recall her talking to some one next to me (although there was no one there at that time) I thought the pastor was drunk in the spirit again and wasn't with it. Then two other people spoke up and said he had visited with Fred as he sat beside him and jumped with joy and began praying for Fred when he stepped out to walk the tunnel. Then his wife too said she had spoken with Fred and laid hands on him and prayed for Fred as he entered the walk...Others joined in the conversation, verifying that this truly was a manifestation of signs and wonders of God that Fred would soon be delivered and freed from the bondages that are holding him down and relasing him from the deaf and dumb spirit. This is truly awesome, others have stepped forward verifying what had been seen and said about Fred.

Because this was so real to those that experienced this wonder that they continued to question me about Freds attendance for that night; several meetings thereafter.

Feb 2-meeting I was prayed for healing for my allergys. I fell in a heap; I could feel that I was gently picked up straightened out and laid on my back all so very gently, then it was like someone gently turning me over and placing me on my stomach. I found myself laying up against the platform out of everyones stepping. I went down more to the center of the altar area. I seemed to have gone quite a distance from where I fell.

DOWN IN THE VALLEY

It all started with swallowing a tendon from a crab leg sticking in my throat and going to ER to get it removed –but it had moved and gone on down.

Second—a few days later I had a severe asthma attack. So I went to the Dr for treatment. They gave me several meds and in-office treatment.

Third—I got excruciating pains in my back. Pains shooting up through my spine to my neck. If I moved wrong away they would shoot.

Fourth now into april.

I get tendinitis in my shoulder down to my elbow with shooting pains on into my elbow and on down to my hand in my left arm. Can't raise it or put any stress on it. The more warfare and rebuking I do the worse things get. It didn't seem to make any difference what I said or done or prayed or rebuked the pains just kept coming. The whole church was praying and doing warfare I was getting very depressed with it all.

Fifth—30th I couldn't lay down and get my breath and had some pains in my chest. I tried three times to go to bed but each time the chest, back and arm pains just worsened and I couldn't breath, just couldn't get my breath. So I decided this wasn't right and I think we should go to ER and get this checked out, this isn't right its getting scarry. The ER and myself and my husband all thought I was having a heart attact. The oxygen helped to ease things. Everything seemed to fit in except the blood tests, all was perfectly normal. After several hours the pains began to subside and I could breath better. They BP was still very high and I was still in severe chills. So they decided to keep me over night and continue the testing every three hours. After many hours all the symptoms were gone and my BP also dropped to normal and I quite chilling and still all tests come back normal. All indications were I have a normal healthy heart. That this was a drug reaction that had been building over several days.

Some came and said we are warfaring in the wrong area lets talk this out and see where we need to move our direction of prayer. I felt whipped, drained, weakened, depressed. Don't know where else to turn nothing seems to be working. That's it, the enemy is attacking the mind to pull you down we need to do warfare on the mind, emotional aspect of it.

Right away everything turned around and I turned around and started climbing back up the mountain and no longer in the valley. Praise God! Thank you Jesus! All is gone cept I still have the tendinitis.

WORD FOR OUR CHURCHS

HEBREWS 11:1-40

I see a large block; it is blue-grey in color—a highly polished stone; like a corner stone with square pillars on each side, plain no design of any kind, but there is an inscription on each side; top, bottom and all sides—FAITH.

This block of stone begins with the third row of pews, down the center isle two-thirds of the way. On each side, right and left it covers to midway of the pews.

Those within the block are standing on solid rock with strong faith and expectations. Interceeding, waiting for the glory to fall. Those outside the block are weak in faith and fear the unnatural and the unexpected. Some with blinded eyes and unconfessed sin and in need of repentance and deliverance.

Until we all come into unity in belief, faith and expectations; there will be no falling of the glory in this church. There is much unforgiveness and hardened hearts of past wounds and deeds pertaining to this building and of each other.

UNDERSTANDING 4-13, 14   Ref: 4-9

This vision was given during wakeing hours, each time; over 3 days. THREE KEY WORDS –third row—center isle—glory

Pews—had no part, only the Bibical number three; nor did the location of where people sat.

THREE—union, approval approbation, coordination, perfection (Hartill) Divine fullness in unity, the number of God; Trinity. (Trerry) Resurrection

CENTER—(core) ; body; mass; meet and work together, the seed.

GLORY—Honor and praise rendered in worship, to enjoy, rejoice, exult, adornment. The indwelling presence of God both physical and spiritual, healing. The changing of our bodies to the likeness of the Lord Jesus Christ. Healing must take place before Revival can happen.

COLORS—INSIDE THE BLOCK—MANY BRIGHT COLORS; MUCH ACTIVITY, JOYOUS, SERVING, WORSHIPING, DANCING. OUTSIDE—DRAB DARK COLORS, LITTLE MOVEMENT; STAY IN COMFORT ZONE, FEAR AND DOUBT.

Outside does not mean they are not a Christian, just their priorities are different.

DELIVERENCE

Curses are placed because I couldn't please my mother with anything I done. I was bent over in the spirit as though bowing to her every command and wishes. You were a burden to her.

Osteoporoses, curvature of Spine – spirit of infirimities. At age 17 your mother put a curse on your spine. She threw a Spear into your back with cursing and hatred, she didn't want you, you were a burden.

Verbal abuse—a black long peace of pipe, with each hurting word the pipe drove deeper into your heart. Throughout your life from a very young child, you were told you were no good, unwanted and every thing you did was wrong, you would never amount to anything; by your mother, family, friends, other Christians, and pastor.

Bursitis in shoulder—the enemy has thrust a spike, like a rail-road spike through your shoulder to weaken and drag you down. To take you down emotionally and physicaly so you can't do Gods work.

Physical abuse—a black rubber hose shoved into your lower abdomen. Some put there by your mother

Asthma—spirit of infirmity. Third generation curse. Great-grandmother. Spirit cursed into by witchcraft, occult, or some kind of ceremony or service. [as he said that, I saw in the spirit: An old woman lying on the ground in a hut like building. She was covered with a blanket and her head and feet were uncovered. I looked at her face and she doesn't look to be ill, why is she here? She is very old but looks very healthy. Then the medicine man with painted face, bells on his ankles, leather slippers and a head band, white with a large white feather. Began dancing, chanting in a sing-song combined with a chanting sound and shaking these noise-makers violently. They were gourds, one with the seeds and the other had holes in it for sprinkling liquids. He was encircling the lady on the ground and sprinkling water over her or some kind of liquid and rattleing the gourds in his hands. But why is he doing this, she isn't sick. The spirit answered me and said; she came to him to receive a curse to take home and impart to one of her children.]

Now at this point the demonic spirit of Asthma began to rebell and refused to leave under the command of the man of God. It rebelled with more force each time he commanded it to leave. Praying through with the audience and continued command of God and the surrounding angels of Jesus Christ of Nazareth; he came out as vomit from a dog.

At that time the Holy Spirit filled this vessel with His Love and laughter. None of these things was caused by anything I have done or said. All these curses were put on me by other people in my life. The next couple days my chest and back was sore from the welling-up of the demon from within me.

While all this was going on, my physical mind knew and understood everything that was and was about to happen and why. The demonic person also doing and thinking and saying at the same time. Two complete thought patterns going at the same time. One can also feel the physical changes that are going on from the demon. You can't control either happening if you are willing and wanting to be freed from this curse and LET GOD HAVE FULL AUTHORITY.

George began this deliverance by openly giving a repentence, forgiveness prayer to me and to God; in proxy of my Mother and Fathers negligence, desertion and abuse.

After all this was over I felt like a very heavy yoke had been lifted off my shoulders. Free. Victory won!

I had been praying that God would send us someone that could deliver us of generational, curses and demonic bondages. Thank you Jesus. He's coming back in July, Yes there is more to be cleaned out. I'm ready and willing. I know there is still more. We got allergies and hearing and I'm still having trouble with my arm, it's tendinitis I still can't use my arm.

EMPTIED OUT

I feel light, emptied out—I can do anything physical I put my mind to.
I feel God has done something so great and miraculous within and
For me. I feel freedom, a heavy yoke has been lifted off my shoulders
Fear has taken a back seat; victory!
I feel my whole life has been changed somehow. I don't know just how,
I just know it has. I can see changes in myself.
I am standing taller, straighter and holding my head higher. I don't
Need to look down anymore, for God has taken the guilt and shame
Away. All that matters is that I obey and please God.
The anointing comes on so strong and heavy, day and night. I just
Set and weep by the hour, of just to be in His presence
I'm so greatful and thank God for His healing miracles. What an
Awesome God we serve

THE GREAT SHIP

I was standing at the <u>helm</u> of a <u>great ship</u>. <u>Jesus is standing</u> at the wheel, dressed in helmsman clothes. I am standing in front <u>facing</u> Him. The wheel is six feet across and made of highly polished, very fine maple wood, beautiful

He said to me; <u>stand</u> there <u>and</u> <u>stay</u> as I have something to impart to you. He said; I will turn the wheel <u>four times</u>, when you hear it lock in place I will then give you a <u>gift.</u>

He then turned the wheel about <u>two feet</u> and it <u>locked into place</u> and He said; I give you <u>Grace.</u> He then turned the wheel again the same amount and when it locked He said; I give you <u>Mercy.</u> Again after a short pause He turned the wheel and when it locked He said; I give you <u>Love.</u> And again the fourth and final turn He said; I give you <u>Faith.</u> <u>Now</u> I want you to <u>go</u> and use these gifts <u>in fullness</u> to the hurting. <u>Now go.</u>

I then felt myself back in my cozy warm bed with my blankets tightly snuggled about me.

Was this a journey??

INTERPRETATION

This is a prayerful rendering by Monica of the 4-13 Dream. Monica does not make any claims to be an interpreter of dreams. Through prayer, these things stood out and by the power of the Holy Spirit.

HELM- of a great ship
Is a great calling or decision

Vessel, size is of great importance in her life-calling;

JESUS AT HELM

Jesus is guiding; He is master of her life

SHE FACES JESUS

Right relationship has been established

STAND THERE & STAY

Double directive; twins
Emphasis to remain in the place of blessing;
Wait for direction; where you are right now
Impartation has not happened yet, building
Blocks for impartation

Usually means incomplete but seems to have
No significance to this dream
Complete as in (N, S, E, W, directions
Encompass all, seasons; winter, spring,
Summer and fall). They are all inclusive
As in turning wheel until complete.

LOCKING IN PLACE

Locks in position, you will know the time
of transition and can no longer go back
to where you were. No turning back; new
level

GIFTS: Grace, Mercy, Love, Faith	These are not the natural but have eternal value. These are the gifts of the Holy Spirit

GRACE – Christs righteousness Spiritual power	(in other words, God imparts them through for others, He is the path to do these. These gifts are other oriented; what is best for them. This ministry grinds the devil into the ground, as with victorious faith; as with the fullness of all the gifts.
MERCY – Kindness and love Of God	
LOVE- Gods love and concern For others	
FAITH- trust, confidence	

2 FEET	Could be time reference; gift could be Imparted in stages; gift LOCK, gift LOCK, Gift LOCK, gift LOCK. Stages appear to the same thing.
NOW	After the faith stage stand and stay for Impartation.
IN FULLNESS	Now everything is right; you are ready; Matured as Jesus was when He came in the "Fullness of Time".
GO (first command)	To hurting; others
GO (second command)	Step out after you understand gifts.

This interpretation is exactly the same as I received as the dream progressed; the keywords. This person only read this dream- unknown person to me.

RING OF FIRE

Dan. 1:7

Retreat, Aglow

This was very different from any other retreat. This one was God all the way. The main sessions were on the Holy Spirit Fire. Yes it was heavy, it was piercing, deep into ones spirit. God ministered to each individuals level, more so than corporatively.

Between sessions, God continued to infill. You didn't want to, or feel like rekindling or renew old friendships or just fellowship and make new acquaintances. Your spirit just wanted to set quietly and "Rest in the Lord". Let Him continue to feed your inner-being. Let that spark continue to smolder and build. As the Fire builds, its beginning to consume things within you. Before you know it you are surrounded by a ring of fire. Soon it is belching flames higher and higher. Now God begins to show you how His fire will be burning away the impurities of self; how He will lead you to use the cleansing Fire to the hardened, and lost souls; those in the dark places, to bring the bruised and the beaten into the light of Christ Jesus our Lord and Saviour. I stand in the middle of the Ring of Fire, I see the belching, leaping flames reaching out to touch someones soul. I see myself standing in the midst of the fire as Abednego, Shadrack and Meshack did, standing there with Jesus at my side.

REBUTTAL

My child, I say to you; you need not to feel guilt from the voice of man. You obeyed My voice at the luncheon, even though they tried to turn your ear to what they wanted to hear. The flesh wants to hear of things joyous and of greatness, of miracles that I so freely give. But they also need to hear My judgments.

You almost fell into their trap but you stood strong and followed My voice. That was not to their liking. My Church is weak because it does not heed My voice and that was not the time or place to testify your deliverance, that time will come. You did good my child, I am well pleased.

It is the time of My people for mending and repentance. Prepare yourselves to receive My glory in fullness, for your time here is shorter than you think. Don't look for the miracles I give to you but seek My Will for mankind.

HEAR MY CALL

I saw in the east as far as one could see—fields of white ripe grain waiting to be harvested. Their heads turning every which way. To the west as far as one could see—the deserts are alive with color, the flowers in full bloom like a rainbow in all her glorious vibrant colors, nodding their heads, waiting to be picked, "yes", it's time; seed pods ready to burst open.

Jesus hovering over, looking down with out stretched arms, calling; come hither my children; the fields are ready for harvest—the flowers are pregnant, ready to give birth—the time is now before the darkness covers over all the earth. Tears streaming down his cheeks as he continues to call out. Hurry my children!

The sky is filled with angels, all clothed in white, waiting, waiting to receive us into the arms of Jesus!

He is coming for his bride!

7-27-00 vision

STEPPING OUT IN FAITH

We all were called forward to the altar to pray for a sister with M.S. now confined to a wheelchair.

I waited for an opening as there were so many people attending the service. We had to move into a place as someone moved out. God had showed me where I was to place my hand and what I would do. I finally got in and placed my hands around her legs, just above her ankles (lower calves). When I touched her the anointing began to flow from me to her like pulsating electrical energy—no other way to explain it.

I questioned God, "what part is this healing for?" as there were two other people already at her feet. And ankles. God said," this part is for her feet and ankles, but I will transfer the healing and send it to her heart. Lord, there was no mention of her having a heart problem". At that moment the intensity of the energy was so powerful, her whole body began shaking with mine and the harder I wept the more intense the energy flowed.

When I shared this with my dear sister, this experience, she said there are many kinds of healing going on in a healing session. Immediately I remembered the whole scene, every moment. It was a confirmation of what I heard.

At this same meeting, over dinner; we were discussing ones beauty. She mentioned she had seen a picture of me in my early 20's and commented that I was pretty. Well I never thought of myself as being pretty. I was always told I was just like my father. He was no good, a nobody, worthless, a Bum and alcoholic; therefore I too was a no-account and no one wanted me around them. I was dirty and ugly.

So that's how I saw myself, I always felt ugly and outcast. All though I never knew my father at that time. When I became an adult with my own family and looked him up the family attitudes remained the same about me. So through life I never saw myself any other way.

Then suddenly out of the blue the Lord brought to mind a prophecy that was told me in 1993 at an Aglow retreat, from a lady that stood up on the platform and directed these words to me:

"You are like a rose bud right now. You are very tightly closed but beautifully formed, perfectly, with no blemishes. You will slowly open to a very large, very full, fragrant, red American Beauty, you are very beautiful, everyone will see you in great beauty".

That's all she said and I had totally forgotten it until today. 8-13.

The lady did get out of the wheelchair. With help walked about half way up the isle than walked about five steps by herself. The next morning she was a totally different person, glowing with the presence and glory of God

GRIEVING OF THE SPIRIT

A community worship and prayer meeting. Being this was a prayer and worship session, I was relentent in attending as I wasn't sure just what it all contained and did I really fit in. The Lord assured me I was to step in; and I needed some teaching and deliverance in this area if I want to be used as God wills I need to step out and be willing to obey in all areas, as he wills.

During the praise and worship there is some prayer requests and some alter calls for deliverances. The first call was for; "to die in self". I didn't go up front for that as the lord has been dealing with me in that, in areas of my life so I remained in my seat and humbled myself before the lord, on the floor where I was. Then later as the prayer request began coming forth; one in particular—prayer for seven teen boys who know the lord but have strayed and are into demonic activities, falling away from the kingdom. All of sudden I'm on the floor in heavy intercession for these boys.

Later in the evening we had altar communion. As the prayers were given by various pastors over the elements and events of the trial and crucifixion, most began to weep softly. When the elements were completed I fell to the floor under a great anointing and into deep grieving, weeping. While there the group sang, holy holy softly, then they began singing another song; I don't recall the name but as they began singing without accompaniment, their voices became together like never before, in perfect unison and then the whole room filled with divine, perfect harmony, loud, clear, singing; yes the angels quire were singing along. It was so very beautiful. I could see the room bulging with the angelic choir.

It seems God is putting me right out in the front lines, each time. I have learned that when he tells me to do something and I begin to move out physically; all fear leaves and God takes over immediately. The anointing his and all surroundings disappear. It's just, God and me; nothing else matters.

THE TONGUE OF FIRE

As I sat in worship by the river side, with my eyes closed I saw; like an open mouth and the tongue was hanging out as far as possible. As I continued to worship the tongue began to turn red, it became redder and redder, soon it was like a flowing river of red hot lava. Swiftly moving down like a waterfall, a fountain of river of life. The blood of Jesus, yet it was the blood of Jesus. "Nothing but the blood of Jesus that makes us white as snow." his cleansing blood will wash the sins away over our cities. His blood is pouring out through His saints, a breakthrough is coming, its very near as time is getting shorter by the hour. This is the resurrection of life. This is circumcision and purification; the bride of Christ.

OF POWERS AND PRINCIPALITIES

Oh God! I feel so empty of words. You know the pain throughout my being. The pain in my heart for all the victims and their families. I feel so helpless. I pray oh Lord you will find mercy for the hearts of the terrorists. For they know not what they do—as they are taught as a child by sanctimonious hypocritical people to hate. May your mercy be upon their families.

I pray lord that you will give strength to all participating persons; family, friends, helping hands, care givers: especially the rescue people as they have a gruesome task before them, give them strength; physical, emotional, and spiritually; for their burdens are heavy.

I see, you God, bringing something good out of this horrible inhumane action upon another human being. I see this as a wake-up call, not just for our nation but the world. Bringing the allied nations together in unity; bringing our governments of all levels throughout our nation. No separation of parties or groups or nationalities, just one great power pulling together toward one goal.

Pulling "the church" together in unity for the kingdom of God. Breaking down walls and boundries. The hopeless and lost seeking security for their future, manifesting the harvest of these end time. Yes, Lord, you are in full control of these days.

I see our life styles changing over night the world over. Losing our freedom in our daily life. More restrictions, more surveillance over our movements, more eyes watching every thing we do and say and write. I see this opening the door to the new world order—easing the entering of the one world currencies, one military, one religion. These things moving into action that have been waiting in the wing for the right moment: to begin infiltrating the nations.

As these prophesies are being fulfilled I pray we will put forth the love of the lord Jesus that is planted within us and leave revenge to the or God. For revengence is the lord God all mightys: not ours. With all this, God is is control and will bring something good from it's depths. Jesus is coming soon—are you ready????

May God bless America.

PROPHETIC WORD FROM GOD

Listen my children, look unto me, fear not for these days that are upon you. I will give you strength for these trials and troubles that are just ahead. When you see and hear of these things: you know my coming is neigh. These days will be fearful with many hardships—I will lead you through these times of tribulation. The things you just saw and felt in your spirit is only the beginning—much more is on the horizon. You will see, and hear and feel more of these terrible things. Listen to my words.

To the church—pray, pray, pray. As you have never prayed before. Pray for your leaders, governments, your nation, yes even for your enemy. The church must unite and pull together and then; I will show my mercy on your nation.

This is the time for your deep repentance and humility. You must humble yourself before me. Trust me.

This is my warning to you. Listen and obey for tribulations lay at your doorstep. You must die in self and trust me totally to have peace and strength during all these things.

Fear not for I am with you always. Trust me: for I am the lord God almighty says the lord God

I saw Jesus sitting in a white chair off in a distance. Dressed as you and I dress. He was speaking to a small group of people. He was speaking softly and gently but yet with firmness and authority, with pain in his voice that came forth. As I listened these are the words I heard him say. Somehow I knew these were a special group of people.

HIS EYES ARE WATCHING

I see his eye is watching us: a very sad tear-filled eye.

How many of his people are on their knees before him: repenting for the sins of our nation: our fore-fathers. Are we in humility or just lip service. I am looking for pure hearts seeking and crying out for forgiveness. A true repentant heart. I am searching. Will you be the one?

COME, COME, COME!

Jesus is standing before us pleading with out stretched arms saying: come, come, come! Come lay before me with your face to the ground. Come in humility, repentance—bring your nation before me that I might find forgiveness and have mercy upon my people. Bring unto thee, unsaved that they too may be at my wedding feast. For I have set the table and the invitations are in the mail.

Come, come, come! Many who just died and many who gave their lives died in sin: because they had no concern for themselves or their future or their nation. Don't be like one of them.

Come! Come before me this day and bring unto me your nation. Your nation is dead in sin: pray for forgiveness. Cry out to me;

I will hear your voice among the groaning.

As I was praying for our country the Lord said: begin to write, for the things I have to tell you

Invitations are in the mail—we-us; bringing in the harvest.

HEED MY WORDS

Church! I have been showing and warning you these many days—you have rejected my warnings—you scorned my words—you even mocked my saints. Now I have crushed the spirits of many. I have opened the door for millions—but I see again you are falling back into your ways of darkness many of you: while a very few are hearing my voice. I will send more quaking so that you will hear my calling. Yes I call many but only a few are listening to my calling. My children my voice will soon grow dim and soon I shall close the door. Are you willing to stand in judgment of the lost souls because you did not heed my warnings? You slid back into your comfort zone and say "someone else will do the work that is needed." Oh! I fear for you as my judgment will soon fall upon the world—sooner than you think. Oh, oh. My child I will show mercy upon you if you will heed my warnings and turn back to me. I am your salvation. I will give you eternal life. Turn away from the things of the world. I am your strength.

DO NOT FEAR

I see among you fear and trembling, I warned you of wars and rumors of wars, pestilences and famines. I also told you that you would not see my final judgments I pour out on the world in the final days. I told you to put your faith into me, not of the things you see falling around you. Are you not trusting in me or are you trusting in the things of the world around you. Fear not and trust in me. This is not yet the end. There is more coming ahead. You must trust me, I will carry you through. I will send my angels to war around you. You are my sheep I am your shepherd. Fear not my child for the angels of the lord surround you.

OH JERUSALEM, MY JERUSALEM

Daughter of Zion: the serpent has trod upon your holy ground, infiltrated among your inhabitants and slithered into every corner of your being. Darkness has covered you over. The world has turned against you. Your future is darkened and dimmed by the sins and wickedness of your forefathers, and of the serpent that now oversees your welfare. You are despised by the world because of your wickedness. Once so pure and innocent: and now so unclean. The serpent now rules over you. But my judgment will soon be your downfall. When you tread upon me, it is an abomination to my father in heaven. I will destroy your pagan ways and I will soon build another holy city and my father will bless it. It will be pure and the light of the world. I will reign and govern you soon, and no man or unclean thing shall again cross over your ground. No enemy shall ever again corrupt the daughter of Zion. No nation shall ever again look down and disgrace you. All the world will know you and come and sup at your table. I am the lord God all mighty. My judgment will soon fall upon all mankind. Look unto me: for your salvation is eternal life with me and you will reign in my kingdom, my new jerusalem for ever and ever. Amen.

Lamentations 1:6-12

HAVE NO FEAR

Are you not walking with me. Are you talking with me, are you resting in me? Then I say to you fear not for I am with you. Do not fall into the scare tactics, the old tricks of the enemy. Call upon me for your strength. Ask me for faith where you lack faith. Continue to intercede for your nation, your leaders. Pray I give them wisdom, knowledge and discernment. I will reveal to them the plan and the hiding place of the enemy. Nothing is impossible with me, just ask and believe with all your heart. I will reveal the knowledge in due time. I have taught you how the enemy comes as a thief in the night, how he subdues, misleads and plays the mind games to see his way. You have a renewed mind, the mind of God the father. Therefor believe and trust in me. I see you crying out unto me. I am pleased and yes I hear your prayers, but I also see the enemy plunging deeper and harder to tear down your armor. Put and keep your armor on and secure it firmly with my word. My name will bring down walls and prisoners. Dave and Goliath. Remember David killed him with only a stone: but it was Davids faith and me in him that brought the enemy down. You are in me and I am in you. And with the father God on your side how can you fail? Therefor fear not I am with you.

I Samuel 17:45-51

CHURCH'S ALL MY CHILDREN

I listened when you reached out unto me and I heard your cries and repentance. The battle is not yet won—but soon I will come to receive you for my own.

I disciplined you very harshly: but does not a father discipline his child if he love him. For a wayward child has no honor or respect for his father. You have obeyed well. But do not lax for the enemy will soon strike again and again. If you look away from me even for just a moment you will surely fall. It may not seem like anything is happening: but I assure you, much unseen by the natural eye is taking place, so do not be discouraged for the battle will soon be won. You will be the victors.

My children, the father is well pleased but do not be weary, do not let up on your warfare, do not look back, only look ahead as your kingdom lies ahead waiting to receive you: and say "well done my children". It will be a difficult battle and many will fall by the wayside, for this is a battle for the strong and sincere in heart. In my animal world, only the strong survive, this is also true with mankind.

I am your strength, I will carry you every step of the way, but you must keep on my path and not look to the right or to the left for you will surely stumble if you do. The hour is surely at hand.

proverbs 3:11, 12

WHO'S TEMPLE DO YOU SERVE

Look around you, what do you see? I see the angel of darkness infiltrating your minds through touch, smell, through hearing and through your vision.

The cartoons to poison the minds of your small children with fantasy and magic, super monsters. To collect cards with super creatures, witchcraft, things that entice the young minds. Video games to hunt down and kill human prey. The bigger the challenge the more exciting, the sharper the mind becomes. The more implanting of evil and murder, disrespect of authority and greed of wanting the things of sin, the fun things in life. These things are a cancer to all ages.

The movie houses, are there long lines around the block to see things of me and my teaching? The television infiltrates the minds with immorality. Clouding your minds through your eyes and ears. Yet proudly on the coffee-table lies the family bible, unopened for months. But it sure does look nice there and very impressive oh yes, lets not forget the most intellectual item in the house. You have two now, one for the children and one for the adults: the computer, they are a wonderful educational tool. You can travel around the world, learn other languages, play games, tlak to each other long-distances, even exchange pictures, make a date, and check in on other areas, you like to do when your alone, no interruptions, for better concentration. Now that I have shown you your daily routine, I want you to think back about my words. "Powers and principalities, angel of darkness"; who controls the heavens of the earth. Do you not think he will leave it free and clean—no—that's not his way, that is his playground. He communicates and infilters this miraculous means through the air waves into your temple. He breaks down your senses for he knows your weakness, for the flesh is weak and he can easily infiltrate your mind-set, especially in your free and private time. Who will know? For man is curious and eager to learn about the hidden things, it's so innocent, what can it hurt. Before you know it: he's gotcha!

Lets not forget the news media, keep them informed about all the bad things going around the world, leave out anything of good, we must condition them to war, killings, disasters, soon they will be so accustomed to the bad they won't give a second look. The magazines, the news papers. We can plant subtle logos. They won't know they are my secret messages. Lets not forget the so called christian magazines. Yes we can plant twisted, misleading stories in there too, just add enough truth so they won't notice.

My children be so very careful what you see and hear: weigh everything very carefully, see if your spirit confirms it, good or evil. When in doubt, ask for discernment, let me be your guide.

Be careful of what you put on your bodies: remember it is your temple of God. Do not disgrace it with amulets, sexy dress, painted pictures. When you see these things they disgust you: they are an abomination to me. So be pure in body, soul and spirit. Are you sitting in my temple on Sunday, and in balaams temple the rest of the week? Do you lust for the things of the world or do you have a deep hunger for the things of the kingdom of God? What are your daily thoughts where is your mind-set? Who's temple are you worshipping in, who are you serving? Your temple; balaams temple; or gods temple?

Ephesians 5:9-17

THE WHITE HORSE

No human on earth has seen or can imagine the kind of fury or tribulation I am about to release upon the earth. I am about to open the scroll of the seals of the four horseman. For these last days. I am about to release the riders of the horses. They will be freed to open and pour out the fury upon the earth.

There will be no place to hide or run to. You cannot hide from the fury of God almighty.

He has spoken and you mocked and rejected his word as mumble-jumbo: saying I have heard these threats all my life: the disciples too, heard these words and saw none of these empty promises come to pass. So why should we listen today of these same words. My foolish people you have no knowledge or understanding. You are like the five virgins who did not keep their lamps filled with fresh oil. Will you not perish? Rich or poor: king or slave, I will show no favoritism. Though you will cry out for mercy or even ask for a quick death: I will not hear your voice as you did not listen to my voice when I called out to you. I will not know you. You rejected me and turned to your idols and other gods, now you can look to the God of darkness. See if his promises will fill your needs, your hope, and your dreams. The time that lay ahead are so terrible you cannot imagine or begin to comprehend with the natural mind. But you will still have one last chance, you can choose to stand with the remaining believers and be slain for my sake by the evil one and have eternal life in my kingdom ever after, or you may continue to follow the leading of the evil one and die in the everlasting fire.

I pray to my father in heaven on your behalf that you will heed to my words: seek my kingdom with all of your heart, before it is to late. Fill your lamp with oil to running over and be ready. Keep it trimmed and filed, as you know not the hours or day I come

Revelation 6: white horse: first seal

MIRROR ON THE WALL

Mirror mirror on the wall
I don't like you at all
You show me tattered and torn
Withered and forlorn
Mirror on the wall
I see laughter and joy
Hidden in those folds
Yes, that face is
Weathered and worn
Do you know that soul of old?
That face in the mirror
Has planted and toiled
For very young and very old
Have you heard the stories told
Mirror on the wallyouth and beauty has faded
Now weathered and withered
Replaced with wrinkles and aged
I look into the mirror on the wlal
I see wisdom, gentleness, longsuffering, love for all.

FERVENT PRAYER

Oh my precious children: I have spoken my words to you many times. The things you need to do and pray about these last days.

My glory is about to fall upon my people: my servants, my faithful warriors, my children you are not following my commands I have given to you through my prophets. Some of you are not on your faces before me in fervent prayer. I can not fulfill and perform my miracles in your congregation until you see and do more fervent praying among you. I have so much I want to pour out over you. I am preparing my servants for this great revival: you are not ready for the grand opening. Some of you are just playing church, so you are only receiving a small sample of things to come.

Listen up, look up, do you not see me standing at the gate. I am that I am. I am sorting out the tares from the wheat. I am looking for pure hearts with sincerity to serve me to the fullest. But I need a whole body and willing beings to give everything to me. Many are not yet ready, some are still serving two gods. I am that I am. Serve me with your whole being: body, soul, spirit or I shall cast you out.

Come seek my face. Come seek me: not my blessings: all these things shall be given you. Hear my voice and obey. I have so much more to give to you, beyond your comprehension. Things unseen, unspoken in the flesh.

Come behind the veil and into my presence. You excel me with your praise and worship and will exalt you.

RECEIVE MY ANOINTING

(church)

Oh my precious ones: you are hearing my voice. Many are obeying my words: but I see many need your prayers and a helping hand to stand strong in faith and believing my words. I speak through my prophets for those that haven't learned to hear my voice. Continue to pray that all my people hear my voice and obey my commands.

I see the wailing and weeping of many. I hear the fervent prayers of my saints. Stay on your faces before me for the coming days will be glorious and trying. I am beginning to release my miracles through some of my faithful and trusting servants. I am anointing my beloved with a greater heavenly realm. So I say to you: seek a deeper relationship and intimacy with me. Enter in behind the veil. My glory is over you now: my angels are all around and about you. Look up with anticipation and as a survivor.

KISSES

SATURDAY

During worship time I saw in the spirit my right hand. As the anointing flowed through my hands they felt like electricity. Then I saw my right hand with a glowing white light outlining it (flourescence type). Then there were a few short flashes of lightning, then there was a big shot of lightning come right out of the palm of my hand. It was awesome.

SUNDAY

The anointing was so very strong in the church as you entered the sanctuary, it was over powering.

During worship I saw (twice) a face before mine. Its eyes were closed, had a small button nose and a small round mouth. The face had bumps on it I thought of it as my face appears. I wasn't afraid of it: it seemed happy and loving. Then it began to move its mouth as though it was throwing kisses. It just kept doing it. I found myself throwing kisses back to it.

Had a powerful ministering lesson followed by an altar call for inner-hurts and unforgiveness. As I was being prayed over I began to cry from deep within my spirit. I could feel and see (like black golf balls) bouncing up and down. The harder I cried the faster and harder they bounced. They soon began bouncing so hard that one by one they bounced out of me. As I lay sobbing I felt peace, overwhelming peace and like I had been emptied out: along with the love and glory of God flowing over me. It continued on through out the day.

3-3-02

As we began worship and I closed my eyes I saw one eye of Jesus, he would look at me and then winked.

WORD FROM GOD

SELF

My daughter—I see your tears. I know your heart. Your crying out to me. I have things in control. I have a plan and it is unfolding before you. Soon the doors will open and my blessings will pour out over you. Your desires will be fulfilled. I will remove the stones before your path. I feel the pain you express to me. I will heal and deliver that pain from you. You are a good steward unto me. I am your lord and savior. You hear my voice and you obey my word. Your heart is pure. You serve me with sincerity even when handicaps befall you. You find ways of working around them. You give your all, even though you feel it is so small and insignificant. It is all great works. Nothing is small and insignificant.

I know your weakness and I will guide you through each and every one. Just keep your eyes on me and reaching out for my hand.

I see your husband and the canny ways the enemy is deceiving his mind. His heart is pure, his mind is weak and with sickness. Continue to reach out to me to help you walk through this trying time. I will give you strength, and wisdom through the days ahead.

I will bring your sisters and brothers in the kingdom to come alongside of you. I will bring your family into one accord.

Look up for I will draw neigh.

vision   3-14-02

As usual I questioned the lord as to whether this was a word from him
or was it my thoughts. As that is surely the things I want to hear. As
these things I have knowledge of in self.

So he showed me the difference.

I set in a large area, void of any material things or surrounding sounds
or actions, total silence. I see myself setting with pen and pad, intensely
listening to the person sitting off aways. Straining to hear every word
and double-checking each statement for accuracy.

                                                          6-10-02

My dear sister and brother: your house has become unclean with
ungodly spirits. You have allowed them to enter into your home and
life. You allow the enemy to over-come my glory. You cannot see my
glory and manifestations with darkness clouding your mind and vision.
What you see with your eyes you also see with your heart. Each time
you open the door to unholiness more enter in. You are seeing evil for
good and tell yourself there is no harm.

I tell you to bury and rebuke those things of evil. Allow my spirit to
direct your spirit to my ways.

The enemy has deceived your mind and blinded your eyes.

I tell you to clean your house that I may reside in love and peace. And
fill you with my glory.

The enemy rebelled big time. He got right in my face and proceeded
to blame me for causing dissention in this household and causing him
to not be able to watch and enjoy things that he like to see on t.v. He
then began to give a list of justifiable reasons as to why it is all right to
watch demonic and witchcraft things.

God also spoke to me about something I was watching, said I have watched long enough now as I still haven't found the answers or explanations I was seeking and I won't find them either as it is work of the enemy. I have told you that humans do not come back from death. All manifestations of spirits and ghost are NOT OF ME. Haunted houses are of the devil.

6-18-02

Dear lord God: several years ago you planted into my heart a ministry for women of broken hearts, emotionally and spiritually woundedness. I have listened and tried to obey your leading steps for each phase. I tried and failed to get it going in churches I attended. Then several years later you addressed the ministry to me. Lord after much of your speaking to me about leadership and I continued to search (else where), you finally got my attention directed to my self and not on to others to do the job. I accepted the responsibility. I have earnestly listened and taken your direction and put many lessons together. I have listened and obeyed your direction as I understood them as to subject matter and waited for each step. I stepped out in faith knowing you were in charge. Lord the enemy has pulled in every direction and tried to destroy and discourage and deceive me and this ministry. I continued to listen and research lessons. I believe in my heart this is ordained by you and each lesson is directed by you. I will begin the sessions again when school resumes this fall. I believe it will manifest into a teaching, releasing and healing ministry. I will have two helper leaders directed by you and a full class. This is your seed planted within me, I will sow the seed you have planted and it shall be watered and matured by your leading and blessings. The enemy will not remove, deceive and discourage me or my class or my fellow leaders.

I declare this said and done by the will of God with your blessings and grace. Lord I ask these things in your holy and precious name, in the name of Jesus.

VISION (4 am)

I saw Jesus going from town to town, selecting people of all ages; gender and race. Pointing to them and telling them to go and gather at a central specific location and stay there until he calls us forth. He went throughout the nation to all towns, big and little, and then throughout the world nations doing the same thing. This was to be finished within three—four days time period, day and night he traveled. He was gathering his people to take us home.

I saw many faces I knew would be there and many I was surprised to see there. While many I expected to be there were absent. I would see people standing on the sideline. I desperately wanted to go to them and pull them in with us, but we were told not to gather in anyone: this was the calling of Jesus himself: not ours and we were not to question or disobey. The groups were surprisingly quite small. I expected very large crowds. As he ascends upward to the heavens he will be calling us to follow him to our heavenly father and home to be with him.

It was like there was an invisible wall, those outside the circle of people: could not penetrate the wall and join in the group, only the ones that Jesus pointed to could get through. The people outside were yelling and crying, pleading with us to take them in with us.

He came as a thief in the night. And the door was closed.

Message I hear him saying, go gather and wait for my coming is neigh. Go reach the unsave. Time is very short. The fields are ripe and ready for harvest. He is separating the tares from the wheat. He need to e out there bringing in the harvest as time is running out. They are hungry and searching. I know the word says he will come in a cloud and call us unto him: not in the manner I saw it in this vision: but the message is the same. Many are called but few are chosen

A WORD

My dear sister: I have spoken to you many times in these last few months. You have listened and wrote and obeyed. I have told you personal and intimate things. You have done with them as I have asked. Some have fallen on deaf ears while others have seen and listened. I will be giving you more intense and intimate secrets of my father in heaven. You will be astonished and have doubts of many of my words but I know you will quesiton and double check what you hear and write. Some will be for your ears alone while others will be directed to your church. You will do with them as I direct you. You are my faithful servant.

The time is very near. Prepare your mind and heart as you have prepared the basic needs for the upcoming time.

Prepare my heart of God. Give me the mind of Christ.

Answer: (Maryann)

He will do the things he told me he would do.

I am swimming in the river, deep water. Diving in from the top high board into the deeper water.

No longer will I be called servant but friend. I will grow deeper and do greater things unto him. I will do the things he gave me to do. It will be successful.

JOHN 15:15, 16

Servants-master=======father-son========relationship   to Christ and the Father.

Friend-mutuality and love. I have chosen and ordained you.

MOTHERS

I saw my mother and Fred's mother and a tall man walking back and forth in the background, dressed in dark gray. Sorta in the shadows of the trees that was in the back of the field.

There was a family gathering, like a reunion, only it wasn't a reunion. Everyone was milling around and visiting in small groups: talking about a specific person. I couldn't hear what they were talking about. The mothers were just mingling around, circling among the people but not joining in any conversations, just observing. The mystery man never made an appearance. I was just standing off to the side observing everything and the actions of the people. It was a solemn meeting.

WORSHIPPING

I just saw myself running to the altar in my church falling to my knees and bowing before Jesus in worship and reverence.

I'm seeing Jesus standing before us at the altar during our worship time.

It's ok lord if you want to use me like that but I will need you to show me something that "I" can see that calls me forward with no doubting of what I see or am to do. I want your presence to fall on each and everyone in the church to follow my leading. If this is your will.

IN CHURCH 11:00am

8-18-02

Prophecy spoken: (tim b.) God is pleased with us. Will begin doing miraculous things within our church <u>in six months</u>. Watch as then it will begin to happen. Things unbelieving. All members of <u>congregation</u> must be clean, repented and in unity. <u>All</u> in unity and clean.

8-18-02

as this was being said; again I saw in a "flash", myself at the altar (above)

VERY STRANGE: PECULIAR.
(THE "SPIRIT" OF DEATH)

Felt very sad and depressed all day Friday and Saturday. Felt as though I was in deep grieving, crying openly and internally. Then all of a sudden at about 4 pm it all lifted. Felt like something had been taken off me, something very heavy.

While watching the history channel on tv," touring the top 10 places of interest, some very unpleasant past history: I felt a presence in the room. Many thoughts running wild through my mind, asking myself what all this meant and wondering why and what did it have to do with what I was going through earlier, with all the crying and such. I'm looking around expecting to see something or someone as the presence is so heavy, I ask "wonder what it's all about? Then to my surprise it answered me and said: "I am the spirit of death". Wow.

I got up and went into my study and got out the little book of "gods promises" and began reading out loud the bible verses on my authority given to me by God.' And rebuked that spirit covered everything in the blood of Jesus: and it left.

Note: it did not say the angel of death but the spirit of death. The angel of death would be here for my husband: but the spirit, what, why the switch?

Now my husband has been in deep depression since our son left sat. Morning of a surprise visit. The spirit of death comes in when the person gets depressed over a situation or ilness. They have given up hope of help or cure. The spirit then looks for entry to fulfill the inner desire to end the suffering. The person feels helpless and sees no hope for themselves and tired of fighting any more, the person is ready to go home to the lord. Satan is more than ready to step in and speed things up over the will of God and his timing.

Self Matt. 6:9   8-22-07

LORDS PRAYER

My dear daughter: not to many days forth now. Yes, he knows he is going home soon. That is why he is hurrying to finish things up: putting things in order for you.

Your inner grieving is a process for the things to come. A spiritual process, as dying is a process. It is the inner spiritual awareness: the unseen, the unspoken spirit, the seeing with spiritual eyes, the things unknown in the flesh.

The angels I showed you in the spirit, circling around in your house, are angels wiating to bring your husband home to me.

You do not know the day or the hour for it is my will.

I am withyou always. I will walk with you. I will hold your hand. I will carry you. I will never leave you. Keep your eyes upon me always.

PSALM 23

W.O. CONFERENCE (SEASIDE OR.) SATURDAY

Teaching was really moving in the various ways of worshipping and praise to God. God loves our worship and praise more than anything else.

There was an awesome move of the holy spirit throughout, in each individual. Then we all went through the ritual of washing our hands before God in a repentance unto him.

I washed my hands of "old self". Many things had flashed through my mind but that was what came out when it was my turn. I gave my old self for a new mind and new heart.

SATURDAY EVENING (HOME)

II-2-92

When I arrived at home I was greeted by a very angry spirit (husband) something was definitely brewing big time here. Two hours later we went to a restaurant to eat: still he hadn't said a word. But that spirit of anger was still hanging around, I could see and feel it very strong. Something was feeding it. We ordered our meal and then here it came. It began to manifest, went all the way, but stopped short of the growling and snarling and began to speak to me directly, accusing me to cause him to not be able to watch tv (star-trek). Something he desired and enjoyed. It is my fault. I am causing trouble and disention between us and in our household. I then at that point leaned across the table, looked straight into his eyes and spoke to it softly but clearly and with authority. Told it to go down and go back where it came from. It then went down and everything went on as though nothing had happened out of the ordinary. I see withcraft and some of the characters as demons. When he watched that program I feel and fight the enemy when I turn on tbn.

God has spoken to me and him about watching unclean things that it opens the door wide for the enemy as he is inviting them in and saying in essence it's ok because I say so and I'm the boss in this house. God also spoke to me about something I too was watching that was not right.

This is not the first time I have been attacked in this manner about this subject. Each time it gets more intense.

SUNDAY EVENING

II-3-02

Husband came in from outside: just walked through the house past the room I was in seated typing. He said nothing nor did he stop and look in to see what I was doing. All of a sudden as he passed by my door something jumped off of him and onto me. I felt it and thought I saw something fly across the room. Was like a blanket covering me, then began to tightly embrace me as though to smother me. A terrifying fear came over and throughout my being. It became very intense and then I began shaking (my whole body) as though something or someone was holding and shaking me. I began rebuking it and pleading the blood of Jesus: saying everything that came to mind: praising Jesus, continuing to plead the blood of Jesus. Praying and putting on more armor but nothing phased it. The harder I prayed and pleaded the blood the harder it became with power over me. I saw I could not fight this creature alone and I dialed sister faye for help. Not knowing if she would be home at this time of night. God had everything under control: she answered immediately to my surprise. I told her what was happening, ask her to pray. Still to no avail they continued on, they were shaking me so hard I had to hold on to the desk to keep from falling onto the floor and the fear growing stronger throughout me.

I suddenly was very afraid of my husband, I don't know why as he has never laid a hand on me, everything has always been verbal. Why am I so terrified of him at this time?. While faye and I were talking and praying I began praying in tongues, that seem to ease them back a little. I told her to pray in tongues too. While we both prayed in tongues they released me and left. All this went on for at least a half hour or so. I felt so physically exhausted and totally wiped out.

I asked God the next day if I passed the test. I felt that maybe this was a test of my strength and faith in God. He said I passed.

SELF W.O.P. RETREAT 11-24-03

Thank you God for the deliverance. Thank you for your impartation of your love. Yes lord I feel cleansed. I feel purified. I feel your presence and your power and glory. I feel your power in myself. I feel the mighty work you have done within me. I feel power within me that I have never felt before. I feel mighty power in my prayers, hey are truly entering into the holy of holies. Thank you lord. I receive your works in me. I pray I will be pleasing and faithful unto you always I thank you for my salvation and sanctification.

My dear child:

You received much more than you can see or feel at this time. As I cleansed your heart I anointed you with my power and my glory and my love to serve me in a greater way, a new way. I have equipped you to do new and miraculous things you have never done before, things you desire to do in my name.

When you speak it in my name it will be done. I will bring to your memory my words and they will be spoken in truth and impowered. Listen for my voice and my guidance and it will be done.

BLESSINGS OF GOD: (SUNDAY SERVICE: RETREAT)

A lady sitting away from me across the isle called me over to set with her. I did not know her. I don't even remember where she said she was from. As I sat down with her she told me that she had a small gift for me, she would get it after the service. Assuming <u>small</u> meant small, and I could put it into my pocket. Which was just fine as we were all headed home right after service.

Well to my surprise this small gift turned out to be a two foot (across) beautiful hand made christmas wreath. She made, beautiful decorated. As one could quickly see this was no small pocket thing. Nor a suitcase item. I graciously thanked the lady.

On the way out of the auditorium again she handed me something and put a piece of paper into my hand and said God wants you to have this. Again assuming it was a scripture. To my shock it was $5.00 Bill. I just fell apart, no one has ever gave me money before. I caught up with her and again through all the tears I thanked her.

When I got back to my room to check out of the hotel, I unfolded the five dollars to put it away and behold there was a total of $20.00. I had given my last twenty into the offering and blessed it to the lord to use to his will. I had only kept out enough to get a bowl of soup on our way home. God is so good. Praise God. Thank you lord!

12-1-02

Why can I not remain on my feet?

You come into my presence with an open heart to receive all that I have for you. You humble yourself before me and a willing vessel. Some of the congregation is in unbelief: they mock and laugh at my workings.

Some of them is in belief because they do not understand. They have not been taught through my word: or study. They do not desire to move forward into the unknown. They do not know and understand my blessings or my glory. They do not come into my presence.

So I show them my presence and my desire to do for them as I do through you. I want them to desire my blessings and the glory that I have for them. I hold all these things to give them: but they must desire and be willing to be humbled, and be ready to receive and allow me to manifest myself through them before the world to see.

Soon and very soon all my people who desire to be used in these last days: will all be on your faces, weeping, before me; you will be naked before the world. The very young and the very old.

I will present my power, my glory, my anointed ones with power and authority in my name.

GREATER THINGS PROPHETIC 12-10-02

My dear child: the things I have spoken to you are my words and they shall come to pass. I have my hand on your direction. I have spoken my promises to you, that your desires will be fulfilled. You are at the threshold. The door will soon open very wide. You will be doing mighty things in my name. You will be amazed and others will also be amazed at the things you will be doing and saying. You will not be put on a shelf. Greater things are to come

12-29-02 PREPARING WORD

My dear child: I have spoken many things to you, these past few months. All the things shall come to pass. I have been preparing you in many areas for many tasks in my works and many areas on your coming days. I will give you the strength and wisdom to carry you through the trials that are before you. Many will be encouraged as they watch you walk in my grace and in my finese.

12-29-02 CONFIRMATION ministry

I have been asking God about my ministry for the hurting women. What was his will as my trials are going nowhere.

He told me: nothing is happening as there is no prayer support: no groups of acknowledgment behind us, there needs to be authorized support and acknowledgment go forth to the proper channels and group leaders before this can be ordained as an approved ministry: and proper background intercessors.

Today: it was announced and "confirmed" that future ministries will be acknowledged and ordained in this church; before releasing them and putting them on the church web-site and confirmed by the church board. This was the answer I was waiting for. I tried to do this without waiting on the lords go-ahead. As it was written and put together and completed by the lord, I thought it was ready to roll, then and now. Authorized persons are going over all the material very carefully, page by page and readying to write the necessary recommendation letters to be presented to the proper channels. When all parties have received their copy then we can go on with the finalization.

SEEK THE BEAUTY

Where has the beauty gone?
Beauty is in the eyes of the beholder
In the memory bank, minds eyes.
Do you see with a childs anxiety?
Are we there yet? Oh how boring.
Have you seen the beauty yet?
Have you laid on the grass on a starlite night?
Watched the shooting stars,
Wondering where they fall?
Wondered what the dippers are used for in heaven?
Where does the moon go when it hides from view?
Why don't people fall off this planet called world,
Those on the other side or spin off into eternity?
Do you see the beauty yet?
Drive off into the depth of the forest.
What serenity, tall stately trees.
Each in there place and a place for each species.
Look around, careful where you step
Over there johnny jump-ups, blue bells, daiseys every direction.
God has decorated the forest floor.
See the beauty everywhere
Off to the mountains we go, up away like a bird.
Looking down upon the world so high.
A roaring waterfall, cascading down the mountain side.
Flowing through the valley bringing living water
To gods creatures, big and small.
See the deer, long horned sheep browsing on the underbrush.
The birds singing as an angels quire.
Eagles souring high above with wing outspread, so easy aflight.

The distant mountain peaks white with glistening snow.
Do you see the beauty
Down in the valleys the valley so low.
The green soft meadows, the babbling brook.
A family picnicking while grandpa is fishing.
Over yonder a bee farm. Lets lay on the ground and watch the work.
Quiet now and listen. A buzzing busy hive.
Here come some with their pouches on their legs
Filled with golden stands of pollen to feed the young.
Others with special bags to carry back nector
To transform like magic into honey we like so well.
Over there in the meadow are some deer feeding.
If we could see I'm sure there are many small creatures
Scurrying in the grass. Look beyond to the rolling hills
How picturesque, such beauty.
Beauty lies all around, see it.

DAYS JUST AHEAD OF US

I see a very large rainbow, very high in the sky and directly over head. It seems to go into infinity on both ends. It is different than all of the others. There is a white pure light that comes straight down to earth, over us. No colors just pure clear white light. In this band of light are people standing as far as you can see in both directions: right and left. All colors of race: young and old. Every one is facing in the same direction. Everyone standing in reverence with their heads bowed in silent fervent prayer. There is overwhelming peace and safety felt within.

You can feel an invisible barrier: a wall of armor in front of us: on one side of the band of light. On the other side of it is total dark-ness. It is so black and dark the feeling is cold, silent, terrifying, death, the unknown. No penetrating light into or out of that blackness. Behind us is also darkness, but it is a normal dark night. This is a very large forest area. The trees are tall and spacious. You can see people (shadowy figures) moving around. Most are single figures. A few couples and some with small children at their side: some carrying babies. They all are walking directly and deliberately toward us. They can and are entering into the band of light. Many fall on their faces in repentance, some have fear and wonderment on their faces: some are weeping: some just come in and stand and embrace with someone.

There is a great movement of God on the way. There is also a great time of hardship and torment just ahead. There is a time of great repenting. A time of continual praying, fervent praying. Keeping your armament on. A time of unity and strength, holding each other up, closeness, fellowship; for our survival. There is a dividing of the tares and wheats. If you drift from God, even slightly, you will be in great danger and trouble and may get lost forever.

People are running to the lord and salvation.

SHATTERING STRONG HOLDS

VISION/DREAM

I was in church laying on the floor. Faye and Koni were praying over me. Pastor and some others were standing at the altar off to the side praying.

I was sobbing and then suddenly I was being pulled (slid) supernaturally across the floor: first by my feet very quickly: then reversed and pulled supernaturally from my head very quickly. It felt like I was floating just off the floor. I knew it was God. Then it would stop moving me and I would again begin to sob. A couple of times I was vomiting as through I was being delivered of something very evil or dirty. This seemed to go on for some period of time. I really was not asleep I was semi-awake. I was standing back watching this happen to me <u>and</u> at the same time I was experiencing all of the action. Sometimes I too was praying as in a repentance prayer. This was a physical experience

When I woke up completely I ask God if this was really him? I heard: you have been prayer "shattering your strongholds: breaking the power over your soul"

THE SHADOW

At class I was in so much pain with my back, I ask for prayer. As pastor Dan prayed for me, we both felt that there was a hinderance, like a wall or something stopping the healing to be received from God. Couldn't describe it. It was just something blocking.

I ask God to reveal the cause to my prayer warrior, or myself or someone to reveal the prayer we should be praying for seeking help for deliverance or repentance for healing. What is the barrier

I called my prayer warrior and told him the situation and ask him to pray and ask God to reveal what we need to do, either to him or through any one else.

Four days later he called me back with what God showed him. He described exactly every detail that Dan and I were feeling, only he described the vision God gave to him.

This is a spiritual thing. It is like "a shadow", same size as. I am. It's as though it is attached to me. It is 6-8 inches from my back. It is there all the time to destroy and to immobilize me. It has no distinct shape. It cannot touch me only speak its wishes. It cannot touch me because there is a armor around me. It cannot go in front of me because of the face of Jesus is there, it has to remain at my back at all times. It cannot come between God and me. This is an evil spirit, to deceive and destroy.

To rid this thing is to fast and pray. Warfare to kill and destroy it. That it can never come back. Healing prayers are not the answer, only deliverance through warfare can this thing be broken, then God will be free to do the healing.

GOD'S POWER

Church was awesome. As the praise and worship started, the presence and anointing of God began to overflow me. I was so overcome with the presence of God. As the worship progressed so did the anointing. It continued on throughout the sermon, altar call and out to my car. I felt God was doing an awesome thing, he was healing and delivering me from this pain and the infirmity that has been upon me these past six weeks. All through the singing I continued in my prayer language. The more I prayed the heavier the presence. Those around me began asking me if I was alright. I told them it was just a God thing. All the pain has left cept for the one main muscle that has been in spasms for days. But it too has to go. I have the victory. The devil has no power over me. I am covered in the blood of Jesus. I am healed.

I was covered by the anointing of God, just like I was at the benny hinn crusade. The time God took the pain from my spine fractures.

As the anointing progressed in me: those near me seemed to be receiving some of the same thing. Our little corner was pretty well under the influence (dui) drunk in the spirit.

The next day (early evening) I suddenly noticed that I had no pain. In my back and was able to move freely. The muscle spasms are gone also. I had a good restful nights sleep without pain and tossing and turning. First good night in many weeks. God is so good! I feel there is a large empty cave, very dark now behind me, way behind.

7-2-03 The cave is no longer in darkness. It has drifted farther back and now is filled with light. The spasms are gone, I still have some bad days with the broken rib. God is healing that too.

GOD'S WORK AND HIS PROMISE

My husband friend again called his brother, and again the brother continues to dig into the past hurts and disappointments. Dwelling and digging into past and lost records, only to manifest some truth into untruth and deepen the hurts and anger, along with resentment and rebellion.

This only creates an irate anger and brooding to the brothers and continues the feuding within the remaining family members, that has already gone through generations.

I was able for the first time to communicate to my husband as to what this torment is doing to him. These same conversations go on each time they talk. Each time the anger grows deeper.

With his broken spirit he listened and received what I was telling him in love and truth, for the first time I was able to draw out the attitude and personality that portrays the inner hurts and anger. How people perceive him and react to his defensive and rebellious ways, that chip he carries around on his shoulder waiting for someone to touch it.

Explained that he needed prayer and deliverance of all those hurts and anger he has carried and harbored all these years. He couldn't do this by himself that he needed someone to pray with and over him. Go to the altar and ask for help. It may take several times of prayer for complete healing.

He ask: how can I do this and get help (this came from God). I explained again he needed to reach out and ask for the help and prayer and deliverance with prayer warriors or we can go to (his pastor) and get help he started to say yes lets go: (I could hear his spirit speaking), but then suddenly he changed character and these words came out of his mouth: "no, I want to keep it all and I need this chip on my shoulder too, I like what I have".

I know God is doing a work in him. God brought him this far He will finish his work. Praise God. Fred is still thinking on the things we talked about, as bits and pieces still come out through conversations, even though they come with resentment in his voice.

My Dear Child: 10-16-03

UNDERLYING LOVE

I see your pure heart. I see your love for me. I have bigger plans for you to serve me in a bigger way. For your desire is to serve me in a greater way. I will move youinto deeper relationship with me. I will have people come along side of you to lift and guide your steps. I will do miracles through you. You will see people healed. I am moving you into a closer relationship with me through your worshipping of me. You will glorify my name through word, through worship, through works.

The little insignificant things you do, you do them for my glory with unselfishness and sacrifice. You touch many lives with your love for it is my love you show forth. Your small deeds and gifts are blessings to others and you listen to my guidance and give accordingly. Sometimes the gifts are not understood or accepted in the manner they are given, but in time they do receive and understand the giving.

You come and serve in simplicity. But every thing is covered with my glory and love. The best wrapping available. A beautiful wrapping the world cannot offer and cannot see. You are of few words because of many rejections as you don't have the polish. That, so many times is just that, polish. Sometimes the dull one outshines. In every way because of the underlying love. The best of the best is love

GRANDMAS HOUSE

Off to grandmas house we go in the countryside.
Rows and rows of white fences, a big red barn.
Here and there a herd of cattle, a field of horses.
Rambling farm houses with white picket fences
Everything neat and trimmed
See the lambs born, new life into this awesome world
Who know what more lurks out there.
Apple pie fill the air. Chickens singing giving
Fresh brown eggs for the morning omelet.
Home made ice cream and chocolate cake for our farewell
Nature is so beautiful
On down route 66 on to the beach we go
God made the heavens and earth and the waters there upon.
He put fishes in the seas, creatures big and small.
Good food to nourish our bodies
Each with their special place in the eco system.
Listen: to the ocean roar. As the waves crash and tumble the rocks
Can you count the sands of the sea?
Search the pool and what do you see?
Anemias reaching to catch a meal. Pick up a starfish
See its many legs, why does it need so many?
The sand dollar what purpose can it have?
Oh how wondrous the works of our lord and savior.
Only God can make a flower with all its specialized parts.
Everything God has made is beautiful

LOVE LETTER FROM JESUS

LIAR mon. 3-1-04

My dear child: listen for my voice and I will tell you truth. I will guide your steps. Weigh the words given to you. You will know when they are mine or the enemy. This is a time of total trust and faith in me. The enemy comes with false hope and a forked tongue. I have your steps planted and directed. Do not stray or grow weary as I am your strength.

Listen closely to my voice. I will not lead you astray or in different directions as the enemy is trying to do. Double check with me first. I am the way and the truth. Remember what I spoke to you yesterday. The enemy has been lying to you. Seek my words. Check the words from other christians not all speak the truth.

SORROWFUL HEART MON. 3-8-04

My dear child: I know your confusion. I know your caring heart. Yes I imparted a deeper love of me within your heart. I can teach you to feel my sorrow as you feel the pain of others. The things that hurt me so deeply: these homosexual marriages are so much of the devil. He has blinded their eyes and hardened their hearts. Soon so very soon I will call my people home and take them out of this terrible sin. Do not fall into the trap of the enemy.

Your husband too sees the truth in all of this though he is unable to express it in full truth.

DOOR STEP

My dear child: time is very near now. He has made his peace. He has made his preparations. He has everything in place he wants to do. His pain has become overbearing to him. He does not want to be a burden and an invalid that you can't take care of him. But also not ready for retirement homes or care centers. He knows he is standing at the threshold of heavens door.

TELL MY PEOPLE PART 1 4-22-04

My child: you have a very sensitive heart you feel their pain, their sorrows, both physical and spiritual and you want to make it all better.

I hear your prayers, I hear their prayers. You know my word, every thing is in my timing. I am healing their bodies and souls. Some things take time only as they release it unto me. When you ask me to embrace them with my love I reach out and touch them, they know my presence. They know you are lifting them up to me. I give them peace and strength. I am with them always. Your prayers are not in vane or are theirs. I hear them all. I answer according to their heart for many are empty words. I hear all of them from the hearts.

CHURCH nov. 5-04

Oh my children come unto me, come one and all, come on your face before your God in heaven. The time is now. The time is so near. Don't lose what I have for you. Come seek my face that I may pour our a deeper anointing and blessing upon my people. I see so much pain and sorrow, and so much distrust and hate. Yes, even among my people, come, come, let me heal your land. I am waiting for you to call out my name, one and all, call my name that I may pour out my glory upon you. You are my servant: you are my disciples: you are my prophets: you are my apostles. Call upon me to release my power to use you mightily to build and get my people ready for my kingdom and glory for my father

CHURCH PART 2

Tell my people: to go deeper into their souls and speak to me from their hearts for the time is now, not tomorrow or later this day but now.

I stand before my father and plead with him to have mercy upon my people. I cry mercy, mercy upon my people; my father.

Now is the time, come on your face before me and repent, repent as you never have repented before.

I am bringing forth change. Change throughout my church: my people yes, my people will be performing miracles. Miracles never seen before. I will again do miracles as quickly and easily as when I walked with you 2000 years before. I will show once again to the world: I am that I am. Those that hear my voice will obey and be used greatly. Others will mock and fall away.

Give me your whole self, body mind and soul, and I will use you mightily. Do not question, just believe and allow me to work through you. All will be great in me: ever so simple or great. Believe and trust: I will be your strength

To my child: I have blessed you and your husband. You both serve me in your own ways. I have answered your prayers. Your husband can come home now, his desires are fulfilled.

I gave you that precious wonderful time together to cherish forever and I lifted off the heavy burden and given you both peace together. That time was so special and precious, and you were the alpha and omega. Thank you lord. You were in the midst the whole time.

BENNY HINN TRIP 5-7-04

I had given up as to going to benny hinn as the person in charge of putting together the car caravan for our church, didn't follow through, so nothing was organized and no reservations or information came together. At three weeks before the crusade I called to see what had been done if anything and if and room reservations etc had been made. Nothing. I knew at this point that it was much too late to find a room within a decent distance or a price range we could afford: so I ask God "if you want us there God it is totally up to you to provide the way with room and finances." And forgot about the whole thing and excepted that we were not going.

One week later while roaming through deals only to kill time mostly as I didn't want to go home as yet as it was early. I heard my name called from across the aisle calling my name. A lady from another church ask me if I knew of anyone needing a room for the crusade. I knew instantly that was mine. Even before knowing any details about where or how much. I said yes, I do. We made arrangements on a timing to call the motel to change the reservation registrations. It was five blocks from the coliseum and $45.00. Was a bigger room than we usually get with bigger $$. Was quiet and had everything all the nicer motels have. When the time arrived I put together on paper everything we needed to know (information) with addresses and parking info. And gave it to my husband so he could be in charge of things, and know the who, what and whe [unable to read] when he read that paper he instantly changed like a miracle had happened he got out the map and got everything straight in his mind and had it all together. The following three days were like magic. God had given us a miracle. He was perfectly normal, on top of everything, knew where and what, got around Portland like he knew just what was around the next corner, understood everything kept up with the service and worship along with everyone, had open conversations, heard and understood like normal. It truly was a God thing all the way. God gave us a special time together.

MY DEAR LORD 6-21-04

I love you so much, teach me lord to love you also in a father figure yes, I know and I can see a heavenly father but to put it in the earthily realm I can't. As I never really had the actions and physical love image of a father. I saw only as the husband portrayal so I don't understand the roll is supposed to be portrayed. I know the fairy tale father and heard how fathers are supposed to be with their childrens relationship but I never had but have witnessed it in other families. So all I have is the fairy tale father image and I know for a fact you are not that kind of a father, so I need your help to teach me.

I know your words say you are my father, my husband, my brother, my friend and my lord. I am beginning to see and feel the other parts but I need help with the father part. I want to think I do but I know it isn't real to me yet. God I want to see you as that person for me.

Give me faith where I lack faith. Amen

MY DEAR CHILD 6-22-04

I see you as my child, my daughter, my sister, my loyal servant and as my bride. I love you as all of those persons.

I see you honoring and praising me in all of my multiple persons, even at times of the father image. Yes you are struggling with that aspect but you slowly are understanding in the spirit realm, it is just the flesh that is struggling. The husband part has a ways to go yet but you have a great intimate relationship with me and I with you.

One day all of the personalities will manifest in all their glory and wholeness.

MY DEAR CHILD JULY 27-04

I hear your heart desires. I am preparing you for a greater service. You will bring souls into the kingdom. You will lead broken souls into victory. I will heal your soul too as you lead others into freedom. I will bring another to walk through the fires with you. They too will receive their healing as you walk together. Your journey will soon begin

You are to attend your churchs retreat. You will share your two major encounters with me. The walk in the garden path and the fall at the w.O.P. Retreat. You will know which one to do first.

8-13-04

TO THE CHURCH

My children: you are not here by accident for I have called you. I gave my life for you and you are giving your life for me through your serving to another of my children in need. Many of you are sitting back and waiting for someone else to do it you are just too busy.

Look up into the trees: what do you see?

The tall straight ones are my faithful and strong unto me.

The bent and broken ones are who fell and you didn't stop to help them up to their feet. These are my children. Who do you serve?

Are you willing to give your life for me?

CHURCH 8-24-04

To my church I call to you to teach my children the ways of the last days. Teach them of my judgments that lay ahead.

May my children be not ignorant of these days just ahead. Many do not know of this tribulation and torment time. They are my sons and daughters with no knowledge. My teachers, prophets, and my apostles: pray, teach, show them my words of truth. They know not because you have not brought my word forward to them. My words speak truth and life of today and forever.

Prepare my children for the days that lay ahead. These days are at the door. Soon I will call my church home, many are not prepared. I show you my judgments I will pour out, before I call you home unto me. Yes, there are more terrible days ahead but fear not for you will not suffer if you know my warnings.

I will bring great blessings upon those who heed my warnings. I will send my servants to comfort and guide your steps. I wish for none to perish because they lack knowledge and are not prepared for these terrible times.

Listen, my people, and obey. This is not a feel good time, this is the end times. Come closer and listen to my words. My words will not fall on deaf ears but ears that hunger for my truth, words of preparation and knowledge to strengthen and trust in me alone and not of mans babbling. Man sees with blind eyes and plants seeds of untruths with false hope and peae.

Your refuge is in me alone.

OCT. II-04

MESSAGE

My child: you hear my voice and you obey my commands. I have a mighty work for you, healing broken hearts, broken soul. And broken spirits of physical abuse. The time is soon, very soon, women of all ages, a loss of self. Abortions and sexual. Will start small and grow to many, young and old

DING-A-LING? ACCUSATION OCT. I5-04

My child, oh my child you are following your spirit as I speak to it. Do not feel ashamed. Yes you are different. You don't follow their ways. Your mind thoughts do not follow theirs of the world, it listens to your spirit mind. You are peculiar to them. You don't boast or judge them, you quietly lean back away, you aren't in their league.

Yes, you are so different they don't understand your ways because of your quietness. They don't know you. They don't come along side to be a part of you. They aren't where you are yet.

You are what they refer to: as "deep". Far out! No just different and sincere and shur-footed and locked into my word. You don't waiver, it is black and white. That's why you are so tender and have such love and compassion for others. You see both side of the person, the world and me. You can understand their actions and see where their heart's are. Some are jealous as they see who you are in me and some fear who you are: so you stand tall and alone and yes some envy you. You are special. You are unique'. That makes you strange in their eyes of the world. You are mine, my child and I love you.

TO MINISTER TO 11-10-04

Oh my dear child, a child of my father in heaven. I will bring you forward into the spot-light. Ministering my word. Ministering to open blind eyes and remove the stones in their hearts by uncovering their ears to hear and receive my warnings.

Words of wisdom I have laid on you in the past to bring forth for this day. For these words of the past are words for today and into the future.

To bring my children closer to me to reach them with words of understanding. Words to see with their spirits and reach deep into their hearts. Written words, my words I have spoken to you: words I have shown to you in the spirit. Words you have hidden away. Now is the time to reveal them to my children that they might hear and receive my words of warnings and change their ways. Now is the time my child. Some of my word will fall on deaf ears. But this is not to convern you. Just trust and obey me.

VISION (awake, eve.)

I can hear a small group of adults: and can see them standing in the hallway behind me talking among themselves. They are here to lift me up. I am standing in the hall talking with three people of the medical staff. There is a stranger in the side room praying over a patient: a man on a gurney: who is unconscious. I am concerned about the man on the gurney and what all the fuss is about. Somehow I am involved with that patient but no one is telling me what is going on and why am I there: and why are all those people praying. Who is the patient?

VISION

Rainbows –double –preceded a thunderstorm

I give you my words. I give you my peace. Hear my voice (thunder) I speak to you loud and clear. Heed my words for I am your light (lightning) and strength. Follow me / me alone for the hardships (hail) I give you now, is only a small taste. For much harder stones lay before you.

What came to mind was where God talks about the huge (basketball) sized stones that will fall on man at the end days. But in reality he was probably speaking about the tribulation time.

My dear sweet child: I shall never leave nor forsake you. Keep your focus on me. I shall be your guide and provider. I know your need and I shall fulfill them all. Your pain and sorrow are but for a short time. Soon you shall be fulfilled with my joy and laughter. You continue to look to me for your needs. I shall give you peace and friendship.

May I have your attention, please

YOUR ATTENTION PLEASE

Lord you tell us in your word that when you set your feet upon mt. Zion there will be the greatest earth quake the world has ever seen as the mountain splits in two. The whole world will see and feel the destruction. Lord in our earthly minds we cannot minutely in reality comprehend the whole world receiving destruction at once.

But Lord you have just shown us your awesome power how this can happen and have a devastating reaction world wide. This quake has revealed to all of mankind, worldwide. How it can all be possible in a split second of time.

May the world now see the truth of your promises. May the mockers and unbelievers see and know the truth that lies ahead. May this open blind eyes and crush the hearts of stone, that they will believe in their hearts and turn to you for their salvation. May this open church doors to teach the word and your promises, instead of their feel good stories for fear of turning people away. May this speak to the teachers, ministers, the apostles and evangelists. You have shown the world in your awesome power. Again you have opened our blind eyes and hardened hearts. Many eyes opened at 9/11 but they soon fell back into their hearts. How many warnings will you give I ask to please have mercy and grace upon your people as you again show your signs and wonders of these coming last days. I pray you will show mercy and grace upon each and everyone having any part in this horrendous awakening though it be physical, emotional or spiritual.

We praise and worship you our lord God almighty.

My Child....

You may not know me, but I know everything about you...Psalm 139:1
I know when you sit down and when you rise up...Psalm 139:2 I am
familiar with all your ways...Psalm 139:3 Even the very hairs on your
head are numbered...Matthew 10:29-31 For you were made in my
image...Genesis 1:27 In me you live and move and have your being...
Acts 17:28 For you are my offspring...Acts 17:28 I knew you even
before you were conceived...Jeremiah 1:4-5 I chose you when I planned
creation...Ephesians 1:11-12 You were not a mistake...Psalm 139:15-16
For all your days are written in my book...Psalm 139:15-16 I determined
the exact time of your birth and where you would live...Acts 17:26 You
are fearfully and wonderfully made...Psalm 139:14 I knit you together in
your mother's womb...Psalm 139:13 And brought you forth on the day
you were born...Psalm 71:6 I have been misrepresented by those who
don't know me...John 8:41-44 I am not distant and angry, but am the
complete expression of love...I John 4:16 And it is my desire to lavish
my love on you...I John 3:1 Simply because you are my child and I am
your Father...I John 3:1 I offer you more than your earthly father ever
could...Matthew 7:11 For I am the perfect Father...Matthew 5:48 Every
good gift that you receive comes from my hand...James 1:17 For I am
your provider and I meet all your needs...Matthew 8:31-33 My plan for
your future has always been filled with hope...Jeremiah 29:11 Because
I love you with an everlasting love...Jeremiah 31:3 My thoughts toward
you are countless as the sand on the seashore...Psalm 139:17-18 And I
rejoice over you with singing...Zephaniah 3:17 I will never stop doing
good to you...Jeremiah 32:40 For you are my treasured possession...
Exodus 19:5 I desire to establish you with all my heart and all my
soul...Jeremiah 32:41 And I want to show you great and marvelous
things....Jeremiah 33:3 If you seek me with all your heart, you will find
me...Deuteronomy 4:29 Delight in me and I will give you the desires
of your heart...Psalm 37:4 For it is I who gave you those desires...
Philippians 2:13 I am able to do more for you than you could possibly
imagine...Ephesians 3:20 For I am your greatest encourager...2
Thessalonians 2:16-17 I am also the Father who comforts you in all your
troubles...2 Corinthians 1:3-4 When you are brokenhearted, I am close

to you...Psalm 34:18 As a shepherd carries a lamb, I have carried you close to my heart...Isaiah 40:11 One day I will wipe away every tear from your eyes...Revelation 21:3-4 And I'll take away all the pain you have suffered on this earth...Revelation 21:4 And I'll take away all the pain you have suffered on this earth...Revelation 21:4 I am your Father and I love you even as I love my son, Jesus...John 17:23 For in Jesus my love for you is revealed...John 17:26 He is the exact representation of my being...Hebrew 1:3 And He came to demonstrate that I am for you, not against you...Romans 8:31 And to tell you that I am not counting your sins...2 Corinthians 5:18-19 Jesus died so that you and I could be reconciled...2 Corinthians 5:18-19 His death was the ultimate expression of my love for you...1 John 4:10 I gave up everything I loved that I might gain your love...Romans 8:32 If you receive the gift of my son Jesus, you receive me...1 John 2:23 And nothing will ever separate you from my love again...Romans 8:38-29 Come home and I'll throw the biggest party heaven has ever seen...Luke 15:7 I have always been Father and will always be Father...Ephesians 3:14-15 My question is... Will you be my child? ...John 1:12-13 I am waiting for you...Luke 15:11-32

...Love, Your Dad
Almighty God

A GREATFUL HEART

MY DEAR SWEET JESUS:

I thank you for my Salvation and being my Lord and Saviour.

I thank you for taking me out of my life of darkness, of pain and sorrow. Lifting me up into the light; peace and joy with eternal life. With a newness of mind, of spirit and body.

I thank you for the wisdom and your glory. For opening the door that I may enter into your presence. One on one. I was nothing; unwanted, unloved. I was a cast off by my earthly family. You called my name and took me into Your kingdom. You taught me to discern good and evil, You taught me how to love one another; how to care and feel anothers pain, that I might show them your love and tenderness. You showed me how to see man as You see them and to look into their heart—and not upon their flesh. To see the beauty of creation that surrounds me—to look beyond the heavenly bodies and into the glory and for the coming of the kingdom which will rule upon the earth, with the Lord of Lords and the King of Kings to live and reign with You for ever and ever.

I thank You for showing me things that are unseen, sometimes; for hearing Your sweet soft voice; for speaking through my fingers in a written word to those who need a word of encouragement or a word of knowledge or just an expression of Your great Love, mercy and Grace.

I thank You so much. I give You all, that I might serve You in a greater way. I praise and worship You will all my being. I Love You Lord.

When I was a child, you showed me the beautiful things of heaven; the mansion, the golden streets, the living water, the twelve seasonal fruits and all its glory, it was so wonderful; how could anyone not desire all that and the rewards You have in store for us.

But now as I have grown to know You—all those wonderful, beautiful luxurious gifts seem so infantile to me now. I will be overjoyed just to be with You and in Your presence with eternal life.

To worship, to dance, to sing, to praise before You, My God All Mighty I watch and wait for Your calling us up to meet You in the heavens.

MY CHILD 7-21-05

Many will scoff at my words. But be in obedience and listen to my voice for I warn my people in many different ways and through many servants that hear and listen to my voice. I do not speak to just one or two but to many. So <u>listen and be in fellowship and you will find confirmation.</u> My warnings are to prepare you spiritually for the things ahead that you my pray and seek my face and be in intercession at all times.

MY CHILD. MY CHILD: 8-10-05

I call you my child as you come to me as a child, simple and direct. You serve me child like. I love to watch you serving me: again plain and simple. They understand it in a child like manner. You may not remember my words as they are written or where they are located, but it's all there, simple and direct, it's all black and white. They hear it and how they perceive it, is between them and me.

I love you just as you are. That's how I made you, plain and simple. I have a place and direction for each and every one of my people and their personality.

Everyone's abilities and character are unique and totally different. I made them that way. You are just perfect. There are Marys and there are Marthas. Don't be afraid or embarrassed because you feel you don't fit others expectations. You fit mine perfectly.

CHURCH 10-19-05

There is a serpent: a snake: that slithers freely among you. He is murmuring untruths and bringing deception in your midst. Causing unrest and breaking the peace and joy which is burying my glory.

I call to the unfaithful and the warmongers unto repentance. Then I will bring such glory and presence into your tabernacle you will not be able to contain it. I will lift the darkness and heaviness that now entraps you. Without complete repentance I cannot bring forth the miracles I have for you. I have not left nor forsaken you

MY DEAR SWEET CHILD: dec 6, 2005

I love you. I have never left you. You are in my kingdom. I have many gifts awaiting for your impartation. You are in a rest period right now. I am with you always. I have many more blessings in store for you. I have only began: don't let that enemy deceive you, he is lying to you. I have thoe things for you. You are mature in me. You have all those things but I use you differently, they will manifest in due time. I use you as your are, not as the personality of another. I use you in you're your church in many way: no, you do not preach or lead, but I use you in a meek, quiet way and they all see me in you.

I anoint you openly, many see, many fear, many do no understand: because they are not there yet. You are a woman of God. You have my power. Yes they see me in you.

I am sending two people to come along side of you to give you strength and support to help you grow in the ministry I am building you up in, to lift you up to give you strength and build your faith and trust in me. The things you do in my name will be blessed and reverend long into the future. You touch many lives. You minister in your small meek way, but I am there and they see and receive my love, my caring through you. You see my child, you are of my kingdom more than you can comprehend. You are a woman of God.

PSALMS 93
AWESOME GOD dec 7, 2005

Through my mourning of my sweet precious kitty, God showed me his awesomeness and power through his creation. First the kitty needed help, needed me to nurse and nourish her back to health and I needed her. I loved her in her sweetness and she loved me in return.

Then God had me read genesis chapter one and again showed me his great love and mighty power. I really saw who God is: his everlasting love, his strength and all his power and might.

GENESIS I: THE CONNECTION

In his creation of man and animal he also imparted a relationship between animal and man. When man befriends God creatures, they begin a love relationship. For God love is imparted in each to share through the caring and nuturing between man and beast. A love affair between God and man through his creations.

MIRACLE OF LIFE

Mrs Robin goes bob-bobbing along'.
Searching for a tasy plump worm.
She tugs and pulls, twists and turns.
AH— breaks it into little pieces.
Stuffs her Beak—flys away—to feed her nestlings.
You plant the seeds, they don't come up.
You water and weed, —Watch and wait.
Anticipation and wonder—excitement mounts.
Alas—they peep through—grow and bud.
Every color of the rainbow and hues in-between.
Did you ever see such beauty—all stroked by Gods Hand.
The Bees check each nodding flower.
Full bodied, puffy type, she prefers.
A bit of nectar or a grain of pollen.
Hurriedly she flutters from one to another.
Many flights she must endure—to ensure their survival.

DAY OF MIRACLES 2-20-06

Kathy told me about her daughters house fire (6 plex apartment). God ask her daughter what three things would she take with her if she had a person banged on her door and shouted "fire get out". She took her three thing and left the building very calmly. The neighbor were amazed at her calmness and ask her how she could be so calm. She told them her story which was unexpected as they didn't know the lord. The entire complex's attics and roofs were gone and damage into the apartments. The firemen came to her and told her that nothing in her apartment was damaged or burned as there was a fire wall completely around her place which saved it. She only had a little smoke smell. The fire jumped over and around her apartment and burned all else. The complex was constructed with <u>no</u> fire walls. God can do anything.

An hour later in the day (self). Was turning into Burger King. I had slowed down and my turn signal was on. Traffic was heavy one car a ways behind me the other lanes were full both directions. As I began my turn another car from the opposite direction popped right in front of me making the same turn into burger king. We both slammed on our brakes and both began to skid as the pavement was wet from a light rain. Due to the traffic we couldn't see each other. We continued sliding directly toward each other. Suddenly I saw a very large sheet of windowglass pop between us and God said "this will stop you". I laughed and said sure it will. I waited to hear the breaking and tinkling of broken glass with a great crunch. Well, we both stopped instantly and there was only that thin space between us. We both drove away amazed. Wow! I continued to thank God the rest of the day. I knew in my heart that if God put that glass there it would stop us just like he said. But that old devil stepped right in and tried to convince me otherwise. Yes I ask gods forgiveness for not trusting him.

Early evening: was sorting and organizing Fayes Sunday school notebook. I have been kicking and screaming about my participation in her Sunday school class. I'm not a teacher and don't feel I have anything to put in cept for the short story and the poems I read to the kids. If that is really adding to anything. I just feel out of place. Like a fifth wheel with nothing to do. Then God began showing me that what I was doing right then was very important and needed. That's why you are there, for Faye she needs your help. You are her overseer

PROPHECY ART H. AN ENCOUNTER WITH GOD 3-21-06

My sister: my sister: I love you very much. I am pleased with your work for me. I have heard your every prayer you have spoken. I have bigger and better work for you to do. You will be ministering to more people in need. I have prepared you for this work. You will be helping people and encouraging them and helping women in distress with childbirth with encouragement and support. I will give you the strength and ability you will need to perform the work you will need to do. You will be doing things you never thought you could do.

Young women watch every move you make. They look up to you and desire to follow you. I will give you your desires. This time of your new walk will soon be manifest to you. You are truly my sister. ************* As the prophet stood before me I soon realized as he spoke directly from God his face changed to the face of Jesus and suddenly the fragrance (the sweet aroma) of God became very evident. The soft sweet perfume of roses permeated me completely through and over my entire being. I have encountered this very fragrance before but never so profound as this manifestation. Oh to be in the presence of God!

APRIL 20-23, 2006 7 PM – I AM LIFE CHANGE

Planned and looked forward to attending the "life changing" classes for three months but had to wait for better weather: after seeing what it did for the youth group that went to it. I too had to have that change in my life. As the time passed, God began showing me some of the things I needed to get healed and I began writing them down as they were revealed to me and in the order they were given to me and the priority I thought they were to be. Knowing my mothers abandonment and hate of me through my lifetime and through her living years: and the things I could remember, and naturally in the order I thought I was hearing.

Arriving late in the afternoon tired and hurting from all that sitting: and now settled in our cozy motel and a full stomach and getting registered at the church on time we thought we did good and had it all together. Oh so little did we know. We thought now all we have to do is get our material and instructions for tomorrows workshop

Day I—they take us into a room with hard metal chairs and people sitting around the wall in the back of the room. We were in the front with them staring at us like we were convicts or something. Well to assume something is just what the word says when you break it apart.

We were asked if given three wishes & what was our greatest wish. Here we go! We had to stand and face the back and tell all.

My wish was to be able to see God in a fathers figure. As I never had that I really don't know how a real father acts. And never gave it another thought just wondering what came next. We get right into the session. Way down deep and to the point, the nitty gritty. For six more hours of sitting and being told what kind of a person we really are (victims) of our own doing. We build our own walls around us brick by brick by brick. By our own choice. The defenses immediately go up and I wish I had never heard of this workshop. I am ready to leave and head out. They are getting into my safe happy box: but that little voice in my head keeps butting in, "you are here for the whole ball of wax": I wish it would shut up, I should have never listened to it in the first place. Ok I will stay a little longer.

DAUGHTER 4-7-06

Yes my dear daughter: one day I will make you whole. Yes, I will cleanse you and make you pure. I will open new doors into your new ministry. You will begin a while new life. A new beginning in me for I will lead your every step. People will take notice and desire your services. You will rearrange your priorities and will refine others for greater service to me. More people will look to you for spiritual help.

Trust me for your total guidance through your response. Seek my face and listen to my voice and step out in faith and obedience.

Humble yourself before me that you remain humble before others.

YOU WILL BE A MIGHTY WOMAN OF GOD
WORKSHOP 4-20-23

Looking forward for several months for this chance to get clean and pure inside so God can use me as he intended. Time to get rid of all the years of hurts and garbage stuffed way down deep so no one will know, my safe place. I know it will not be easy to let go of the things we want to hang onto. We can continue in our pity parties.

It was the most difficult thing I have ever done. Yes I knew in my heart that I had to do this and God wanted to clean house. It was pure hell. But I am so glad I obeyed. I am now free and I feel pure inside. I feel like a true child of gods.

TRUTH OR CONSEQUENCES
PART ONE ASK GOD 5-5-06

Well—it was shallow, only about eight feet deep and about ten feet wide. Was hand dug in reddish clay. The bottom was hard and firm: covered with a layer about four inches with small round rocks: all about the same shape and size: there was about two or three inches of water covered the rocks. It was solid with the rocks no bare spots, it was easy to stand on them. They were all shades of browns some were very light, amost a white. The water was very cold and clear as crystal. It seemed to be coming from within the ground like an underground spring, but you couldn't see where it was coming in from, it moved slowly and gently. Jesus was standing (wading) in the water also. He picked up a rock, looked at it and tossed it up and down in his hand and gently dropped it back into the water. He then picked up another one and continued to do the same, smiling sweetly the whole time, not speaking a word.

PSALMS 51:1-11

Sees me with a pure sincere heart rivers of flowing water

PART TWO THE GARDEN

I walked through the gate and down the path to the light. Knowing I would find Jesus there. There were many beautiful flowers. Lots of sunflowers: tall ones, short ones all looking at me and nodding their heads as though cheering me on. Jesus took out a tape: a very long tape, it was white couldn't see anything on it. He then handed it to another. He again reached down and took out another tape (ribbon like) it was a red one and put it aside to look at a later time. He said I am missing a lot of important things that he wants me to have and know: spiritual weapons. Come, take and receive what I have for you to grow and give to others in your ministry. Psalms 51:12-17

I JOHN 4:4 he that is in me is greater than he that is in the world.

I am with you always I shall never leave nor forsake you.

BACK TO THE GARDEN 5-9-06

Another walk into the garden: sunflowers are bigger now and so many more of them. The path is very wide and flowers everywhere. All colors, all kinds, all sizes and shapes. It is so quiet and peaceful jet there is a lot of joy and happiness. Can't hear it, you just feel it Jesus and I are just enjoying each other and all creation that surrounds us. We stand at the endge of the pool: the water is crystal clear, cool and ever-so pure. Fish swimming around and around, ever so gracefully and effortlessly: beautiful water lilies: I too am swimming with the fish. First there were few fish now there are many: so many there is hardly room to move. All sizes: there are smaller gray ones and large black ones.

I hear: "you are fishers of men." I see Jesus standing and looking down into the water and saying "well done my faithful one" his arms are outstretched toward me. And he is smiling.

GARDEN MINISTERING TO MANY PEOPLE
WALK THROUGH THE GARDEN

Another walk with Jesus through the garden. This time we are looking for any weeds or thorns that may have crept in. Over there. Look there seem to be some berry vines started. They are just seedlings beginning to sprout. I quickly pulled them up by the roots and threw them at the feet of Jesus along with the hand that brought them.

The garden today is all low (ground cover) flowering plants. Many kinds, many colors some never seen before. They are like stepping stones with little paths between them. Many different shapes. So peaceful and quiet. The song birds are everywhere. Yes many different kinds of butterflies. It is a beautiful day the deep blue sky with whispy clouds that seem to float by aimlessly: a gentle warm breeze. It is warm and so much peace and soft perfume in the air. The farther we walk the smaller I seem to get. I am now a little girl again about ten years old. Jesus is holding my hand as a father holds his little girls hand as they happily walk along together. He tells me I am his little girl.

New baby christians repenting & receiving salvation

ABOUT ONE HOUR EACH MAKE NOTES
eyes closed
SOUL CLEANSING

PART I ASK GOD
1 - SHOW ME MY <u>WELL</u> (box).
2 - SHOW ME MY ROCKS (blocks)
3 - TAKE <u>ONE</u> ROCK: SEE THE LIE.
4 - TURN IT OVER: SEE THE EVENT (ROOT).
5 - ASK GOD TO <u>PULL OUT</u> THAT ROOT.
6 - ASK GOD TO SHOW YOU TWO SCRIPTURES.

Do only one or two rocks at one sitting.

You can move on to the next rock or do a little at a time.

You can do this over and over as you wish.

Psalms 51:6-10 Isaiah 33:2, 35 John 7:37, 28 / 8:31,32 Mica 4:9

VISION
PART TWO THE GARDEN PATH

Open the gate: walk into and down the path to another garden gate. While walking, what do you see: smell, on your way. Look for Jesus. Do you see the light, is it bright? Walk into it: stand there: absorb it, feel it, feel the presence of Jesus. Let him embrace you. With his presence continue on your walk: observe everything on the way. Describe (write) every thing down; what you see and what you feel. Soon you will see a high fence: find the gate and walk through it: close the gate after you. Listen to Jesus as he talks to you. Walk over to the pond. See the clear blue water: look into your face, yes your reflection, ask God what does he see. Ask God what his plans are for you. Bask in his presence. Don't rush away. Take your time, all you need. You have entered into the holy of holies: the throne room of God.

MY DEAR LORD PSALMS 27 5-12-06

Thank you Jesus for examining my heart: for changing me, for you cleaned deep within me: you have taken away all of my garbage: yes, I now feel so empty and light, like I am floating endlessly. Yes, you have surely changed me: I now can serve you in holiness and truth.

I see also a change in my husband. Again I thank you. I know the prayers flooded the heavens for him. I thank you for the beautiful peace within me: and the rest you have bestowed upon me at this time. Such peace, such glory and wonder. I know you are still healing and filling me and there is so much more ahead for me. Right now lord I feel lost—no not of you, but of self as to what I am to do.

We are walking down the garden path again: in the peace and the quiet. We are just walking, not talking, we're just walking slowly toward the pool enjoying each other and your awesome creation all around us.

"Draw me nearer to you, I want to know you music more." When we arrived at the pool: it is just you and me.

Now we are sitting on the throne. It is very long: room for many. The room is very lighty and bright and white granite. The room is full of angels, they are singing softly "glory, glory to the highest". Some are circling over and around my head as I sit and humble myself before him. I grasp his legs with all I have in my physical strength, as suddenly the ark of the covenant appears off to the right. Such brilliance: gold so bright as I have never seen. The cherubims sitting and worshipping on top of the ark. They too appear to be clothed in glowing golden robes it almost becomes too bright to look at. It is just glowing bright but yet soft: everything seems to be taking on the golden glow.

The angels are singing "glory, glory glory to the highest. To the king of kings and lord of lords. God almighty of all the universe"

Even the angels bow down and honor you as they sing "holy, holy, holy, lord God almighty"

I just feel I am waiting upon you for my next assignment. I have peace: inner peace about myself, my husbands health, and all things that surround my life at this time. Oh lord I just want to be in your presence just you and me—alone surrounded with heavenly angels glorifying praising and honoring you. Draw me closer to you I want to <u>know you</u>. I wait upon the lord. For he is my rock and my shelter. He is the one I will serve with all my heart, soul and body. Seek his face; your face shall I seek.

MESSAGE

I hear him saying, go gather and wait for my coming is neigh. Go reach the unsaved. Time is very short. The fields are ripe and ready for harvest. He is separating the tares from the wheat. We need to be out there bringing in the harvest as time is running out. They are hungry and searching. I know the word says he will come in a cloud and call us unto him: not in the manner I saw it in this vision: but the message is the same. Many are called but few are chosen

RAPTURE
VISION (4 am) 6-19-02

I saw Jesus going from town to town, selecting people of all ages, gender and race. Pointing to them and telling them to go and gather at a central specific location and stay there until he calls us forth. He went throughout the nation to all towns, big and little, and then throughout the world nations doing the same thing. This was to be finished within three—four days time period, day and night he traveled. He was gathering his people to take us home.

I saw many faces I knew would be there and many I was surprised to see there. While many I expected to be there were absent. I would see people standing on the sideline. I desperately wanted to go to them and pull them in with us, but we were told not to gather in anyone: this was the calling of Jesus himself: not ours and we were not to question or disobey. The groups were surprisingly quite small. I expected very large crowds. As he ascends upward to the heavens he will be calling us to follow him to our heavenly father and home to be with him.

It was like there was an invisible wall, those outside the circle of people: could not penetrate the wall and join in the group, only the ones that Jesus pointed to could get through. The people outside were yelling and crying, pleading with us to take them in with us.

He came as a thief in the night. And the door was closed.

HEALING HANDS 7-7-06

Friday night service I was hurting and depressed. Pastor took me by the hand to the front for prayer. As I lay on the floor I felt like "a very flat large rock was laying on my abdomen. It was there for a long time and became heavier and hotter as time went on" then I felt "two hands: like they were kneading bread: from the base of my rib cage up toward my neck: gently and slowly evenly both sides together. This too lasted for quite awhile. Then I heard:" your healing has begun: I claimed it and thanked God for it. I have been asking for a long time for my hernia, asthma and allergies to be healed and my spine. I felt for sometime now that I would receive my healing this year: by years end.

CONFIRMATION:—

Faye—on her way home from church she heard God say in a very loud voice: "continue praying for Jessie for her continued healing.

Pastor Jackie—also received the same message.

MY CHILD 7-26-06

I see a great moving of my spirit. They will get to know me not just about me. I will change lives. I will remove the scales over their eyes. I will be in the midst. I will teach them new things.

Thank you Jesus. It is so exciting that I have my peace and joy back. Those two dead months without your presence were so lonely and frustrating. The enemy had such fun trying to destroy my relationship with you and me. I knew my victory was around the corner. Thank you for your presence. Thank you for opening new doors. It is so exciting to see what we will do together.

SUNFLOWERS 8-2-06

There are two rows of sunflowers. Mostly red ones: some yellow, all about the same size. Setting by the pool swaying gently in the wind.

Ripples on the pool like gentle rolling swells. The flowers are thirsty. They need a drink. You are standing there with arms outstretched. Come my children, drink of this water and you shall thirst no more. I am standing in the front, kind of to the side, watching asyou give them drinks of your blessings.

THE POOL: 8-7-06

Standing by the pool with Jesus. Water is crystal clear, soothing, temp is just right. Water begins to ripple around our feet. Nothing in the pool of water: just crystal clear water about ankle high. Faces beginning to show like looking into a mirror: happy smiling faces. Jesus is smiling compassionately back at them. These are my children.

THE GARDEN 8-15-06

Jesus and I are standing and watching all the flowers gathered together in the garden. Big and small, tall and short: all standing and dancing, singing, rejoicing, laughing. Jesus is smiling and saying: well done my child. I can see more coming far off in the distance.

8-29-06

My dear sweet child: I will guide him safely and peacefully. I will comfort and give your strength. I will be by his side. I feel your grief as I felt when my dear friend lazareth died. He will have no fear and no pain. Confirmation given by carolee: 9-3-06

TRAVAILING 9-1-06

I am holding him in my hands, have no fear, have no grief. I give you both peace and strength. He is in good hands, my hands

---

VISION DES ALATE

I am back in the garden, this time I am just looking on. A garden full of wild flowers, all different kinds and colors and sizes. Some small blue bells bowing their heads as though in prayer: tall blue batchelor-buttons bent over as in travailing. Sunflowers encircled one that has fallen. Standing in silence, heads bowed. A small group off to the right side: all white tall stately flowers: singing softly with heads lifted upward to heaven. A small young group of tiger lilies entwined together, swaying and smiling as they humm softly, off in the distance.

There is no weeping just silence and the sound of soft sweet music in the background

Jesus is walking around and through the small groups, touching each one on their heads and blessing them

I am walking down the path again. It is a lonely and dirt path this time: no beautiful plants. As I approach the gate, it too is drab with no beautiful plants. Looks desolate. When I enter in Jesus is standing there waiting for me. We walk in silence to the pool. It is dark, no life in or around it. The beautiful crystal clear water is gone, it is still. Where are all the flowers? It is dry and dusty, the plants are scrubby and straggly. The vegetation is sparse. No butterflies or birds. No singing: it seems so liveless.

God I can't serve you in this realm, it's so dead. I am with you. I will walk with you through this time of distress and desolate time. Standing together, holding hands and weeping in this desolate place.

I see rising a ranbow, like the sun off in the far distance. As it rises it comes closer casting a cloud like shadow as it passes over. As the shadow travels along the flowers are popping up everywhere in full bloom in all their splendor. Flowers everywhere, all colors all sizes everything has come into life again. The flowers are like they are dancing. The water is crystal clear again. We can see our reflection again. The birds are singing. The butterflies have returned.

Jesus is smiling again as we walk through and around the flowers

HELPING HANDS 9-15-06

I ask for help financially and healing hands for the hurting and abused souls. Ans—psalms 21 received check

My dear child I see your needs. I will supply your needs. Do not fear for I am with you always. I will give you your desires.

The time is soon, very soon. I release him to you lord.

PRESENCE OF GOD 9-16-06

The presence of the lord was so very strong. While sitting in a restraunt eating lunch. The presence became so much stronger. I then sensed this was an angel of the lord, this was for Fred. He continued talking about the situations of the middle east and the angel just continued to stand there and minister. I ask it not to take my husband home while he was driving. It remained well on into the afternoon, then left. In fact I got the whole day mixed up and thought it was Sunday.

9-19-06

I am seeing myself in much meditation sitting in quietness, stillness, waiting upon the lords direction, in total peace and tranquility: the presence of the lord. This time is very near.

Growing in intimacy with the lord: hearing more of his voice: to humble myself, to die to self, to be a better steward and warrior. Spending much more time with him: meditation.

9-21-06

My child, I hear your plea for help. I am with you. I will supply your needs. I have seen your sacrifices. I have seen your gifts, and I see your heart, it is pure. I will give your knowledge as you have the wisdom to master these studies, it is surely I that speak these things.

THE LONG WALK 10-3-06

I see my husband walking down a long green-grassy trail through the woods. He is walking side by side with another man. They are just slowly strolling along peacefully: talking about man stuff. They are walking away from me: way off in the distance. The trail looks as though it just keeps going up and over the hill top. It is just an ordinary woods lots of open space beneath the trees: like we have around this area: open and quiet, just the souds of the woods: crackling of dry limbs as the deer passing through, birds talking and calling out to each other. They appear as though they have a place in mind to go see.

THE FOUNTAIN 10-3-06

As I walked the path to the garden gate it was quiet and everything was very still. When I opened the gate, Jesus was standing there waiting for me. He took my hand and we walked over to the pool.

This time the pool has a fountain in it. A tall pedestal with a large bowl on top. Water was flowing from a pipe in the center, ever so quietly into the bowl. The water flows gently and evenly over the edge of the bowl completely around it and into the pool. The water ripples ever so gently out and to the edges of the pool, softly, peaceably.

Many flowers are standing together as if "at attention", they completely surround the pool. All kinds and sizes, yes and colors: quietly listening to the water. "The living waters". Jesus and I are standing together in the midst. They are all looking at us and listening to see what we have to say. Jesus is wearing a long white robe today.

The edge of the water (pool) is surrounded with white water lilies. There are beautiful butterflies in the background, hovering over the flowers, they are the music, softly playing in the background.

(Is Jesus showing me what he has for me in the future?)

WEDNESDAY did not come to pass yet 10-4-06

I see myself standing before the congregation at the w.O.P. Retreat. God has something for me. To impart to me. I receive that word.

LITTLE GIRL 10-5-06

I ask Jesus to hold me as he did as a little girl. He said I am his little girl as I come to him as a child. I love our walks together. You teach me so much of your creations. One day will you show me the heavens. ---- ---- My father has many mansions: one is just for you to dwell with him with everlasting life. With all the things you love and filled with such love and compassion. The sun is for your light by day and to warm and nourish your bodies and the plants of the earth. The moon is to light your way at the night and control the oceans and the seas as the roar with the tides the stars are as angels dancing and rejoicing with the saints in heaven and on earth. The winds the air you breathe and to clean the earth of its own brokenness and to bring my glory the clouds bring the rains to refresh the land and water my creations of the earth. The oceans roar as to bring my word with power and living waters and feeds the fishes of the seas. All these things I do for you and your needs

CHANGE LIVES 10-10-06

My dear sweet child: I have shown you many things lately in our garden walks. These things are your future. They will come to pass soon, very soon. Yes you are my little girl. Your trust and faith is like a child. You follow me like a child. I use you in a childlike manner of love, and trusting faith, because of your childlikeness. People look up to you and listen. You come in meekness, and certainty: with, "that's how it is the word says so. You don't shout or blame you just tell it like it is. You touch hearts and change lives. They listen, they hear what you say, they watch and they change. You don't remember the scriptures in their entirety but they know what you tell them is truth because they see me in and through you. Right now your load seems heavy and overwhelming but the end is near. It all will fall in place and flow as living waters I love you my child.

HOPELESS 10-17-06

My dear child: I see your pain, I see your worry: give your troubles and worries to me, my yoke is light. I will supply your needs. Trust and believe in me. Trust and believe. I will supply your needs.

Lord it all looks so hopeless and unreachable. Yes, you told me to ask it in your name. You told me to seek and I shall find. You told me ask and it shall be given. You told me you shall supply all my needs but it all seems out of reach. ---------------------------------

Ask—trust—believe—I will supply your needs. Psalms 91

GRIEVING 10-25-06

My child my child: I see your pain. Give it to me that I may fill you with my joy. It won't be much longer as his pain is getting unbearable to him. He is seeking my help to take him out of this pain. He is worried about you but he knows your children and myself will be at your side. He has some unfinished things he feel he needs to do yet to prepare the way to make things easier for you. -------------------

I ask Jesus to go back to the garden for a walk as that is a happy place and full of peace. But Jesus keeps showing the scene of the fallen sunflower [unable to read] and the people gathered around, singing and praying. The heads of all the flowers are bowed down as in reverence. Jesus and I are just standing in silence, watching over the fallen one. We walk over to the inner circle and there is nothing there, it's gone. All the flowers heads are now raised upward and looking to the heavens. The birds sitting in the trees are again singing softly, joyfully.

THE GARDEN BENCH 11-01-06

The gate is more beautiful than ever before: white archway with red roses clinging over it. There is a bench now setting by the poll: we go over and sit there and just rest in the quiet and peace: just Jesus and I in silence. It's so peaceful. Jesus holds me as we watch the crystal clear water with gentle ripples as they walk across the waters top. We sit and weep together as he holds me in his arms. The flowers are all just standing there in all their splendor and glorious colors and smiling faces on everyone and gently swaying with the gentle breeze I give to you my peace and strength.

PSALMS 91

DEAR LORD JESUS 11-14-06

I thought our golden years were to be happy and enjoying the things we dreamed about, we built together in our life times as one. Enjoying our children and grandchildren. Being together loving each other and sharing our good times, reminiscing the good old days. Yes, lord you didn't promise us there wouldn't be hard times or sad ones. But why must we lose all that instead of sharing and loving. We are separated by physical and mental illness. I know this is not in your plans for our olden days. Instead of happiness I just see sadness and sorrow upon our faces. Why God why?? It can't be a time of testing our loyalty or love, those trials have come and gone. It is only you and your strength that carries us through these times.

You have passed all the tests of your times together. You are now ministering to your family as loving parents, through your devotion to each other and your faith through me. You see through the pain and sorrow with my love to each other. Your children see that too even though they do not fully realize that at this time. Out siders too see that even though you see others carrying many more and so much heavier burden s you feel thankful and blessed that your burdens are so few and light. Even the negativeness around you: you still have a deep love for your husband and compassion for his inabilities.

You have not abandoned him, you have stood firm and true even in the hardest of days. You are truly a child of God, I too stand by your side.

HOW DO YOU SEE ME 11-20-06

My dear child you are my servant. You hear my voice and step out into new and fearful situations. I bless you abundantly when you obey; as you know. I have much more work for you to do. -----------------Yes lord I can see changes in myself and I know they are not of my doing. ----------------- You are beautiful, you are my little girl. You are overcoming fearful obstacle [unable to read] the enemy has placed before you. You are seeing, hearing, and speaking out in obedience and confidence. You are trusting and believing me more. I will continue to use you in your childlike way. I have others to perform in the bold actions. You are subtle and quite reserved ways. That is sweetness to my eyes and ears as your compassion overpowers them through my love in you. You don't need to speak or be boastful, just be there. You minister through your presence: something like paul did as he would wlak through the crowds.

NOT EMPTY WORDS—3 PM 11-20-06

Fred: I feel like I'm going to die. I think I am going to die.

Lord's voice: those are not empty words. Reply to him with my words: "to be absent from the body is to be with the lord. You have nothing to fear as I go to a better place."

By replying in that way he will know that you have accepted the fact and already know it is near.

Fred: is that so? I hope so. His reply was with fear upon his face.

COME, COME MY CHILD 11-24-06

Come, come to the garden gate that we may walk and sit together. We go to the bench by the pool, just sit in silence: surrounded by peace, wonderful beautiful peace of the many beautiful flowers and their soft heavenly fragrance such serenity and beauty with awesome peace beyond understanding: even the water is tranquil. As far as I can see: flowers beautiful flowers: like a blanket covering the earth. I feel great peace as the blanket is covering over sadness. There is a brightly colored rainbow directly overhead. There are no birds to be seen they are all sitting in the trees, quietly, just moving around to get a better view of things.

MY CHILDREN: (church) 12-4-06

Your days ahead will be harder than ever before, as the enemy will be in every doorway every corner everyplace. You will be attacked from all directions: your homes, your family, your work and your churches. Your governments will become your enemy: but I am your lord, I am your savior, I am your peace. Keep your eyes upon me at all times. I will guide your steps, I will guide your family and your homes. Do not sway, do not look to the left or the right, do not look to others but to me only. I will protect, I will surround you with guardian angels for your nation is corrupt and it too will fall. Pray and fast as never before, for soon, very soon I will call my people unto my father in heaven. Only the elect shall enter in for the terrible times lay ahead.

THANK YOU LORD ------------------12-17-06

I thank you for giving me direction, showing me what to do, how to do it, and for whom. It is such a blessing to see the results, the joy it brings to another. But lord they are not to know that it came through me, as it is from you God, you provided the gifts and directed where they were to go. It is you God, not I

My dear sweet child. As you listen and obey me I will guide and direct you into deeper and bigger ministering., For me. You will see more and more results and receive more blessing as you move into a deeper relationship with me you will be amazed to some of the results. Others will awe at what they see. Things you do now with caution will become natural without hesitation. Keep seeking me and your eyes upon my will.

I will direct your ways.

PSALM 23

TO OUR CHURCH 12-20-06

I see a great spirit of fear that has overcome many of the younger adults. Fears of the future, the unknown in their daily lives and also for their spiritual walk. Hesitating to give all of their self to God: for losing some of their pleasures. Some are filled with doubt and uncertainty that God will really change their life: while others aren't ready to take that step as they would lose their status in their social circles and take on the label of radical christian.

There are also spirits of bondage, error and jealousy. The strongmen need to be sent back where they came from, the pits of hell. If I can't be—if I can't do—then why should I care what happens in this church body. He said—she said—they hurt my feelings. Why do they expect me to do it their way, or do it all myself.

Love: where is your love. God says "love one another as I love you". God does not care how they look, or dress, or fix their hair or their unusual actions. No: God will do the changing in them you don't need to do that: as they grow in the lord things will fall off and new things will appear. It is not for you to call the changes on them, that is God's work

I have great things planned for your church body. I will manifest more of my gifting, yes: some will even seem strange and unbelievable on the surface but you will discern my workings. There are many hidden workings that I will bring to surface. They shall not be judged except by my spirit within you. I will take over more and more of your services that I may do my work in you and through you. I will bring in the hungry and take out the unchangeable.

You have taught the tribulation times, now I say teach the glory that awaits at the door for my second coming. Teach my ways and seek me with your whole self, body, spirit and soul. Open your hearts and receive all I have to give you. Remove the scales off your eyes that you see and search only me. Open your ears to only hear my words and listen for my small voice that you may hear and obey my directions. Seek, trust and obey. Open your heart that I may have all of you, for the time is short.

ANTICIPATION 12-26-06

Jesus and I are sitting by the pool in the garden. Very brightly colored flowers are everywhere. They seem to be dancing with joy. Many more are coming down the mountain side, running, singing. We are surrounded with flowers, tall ones, short ones.

Sunflowers are gathering into small groups all around us. Smiling, laughing, rejoicing. I will open new doors. I will fill the rooms with the hungry: hungry to hear my word. You will find peace and joy everywhere you look.

You will get a great following, as they look up to you for guidance. You will give me your whole self. You will walk and talk in my glory. I will impart new things within you. You will wlak in wonderment. You will witness miracles as lives change. I will guide your steps. I will supply your needs. Keep your focus on me. Do not look right or left but directly upon me. Yes, you are standing at the door to be opened soon, very soon.

The anxiety and anticipation you are sensing is about to be fulfilled. I am your lord and God. Let go and let me, that I may work and fulfill your p urpose.

The uncertainty, the frustration you sense is learning patience: waiting upon me. It's all in my timing. The more you are in my presence the stronger your anointing will become and the deeper your love will grow in me.

Dear Friend;

How are you? I just had to send you a note to tell you how much I care about you.

I saw you yesterday as you were talking with your friends. I waited all day, hoping you would want to talk with Me also... As evening drew near, I gave you a sunset to close your day and a cool breeze to rest you, and I waited...You never came...Oh yes, it hurts Me but I still Love you because I am your friend.

I saw you fall asleep last night and I longed to touch your brow,.....I wanted to rush down so we could talk...I have so many gifts for you! You awakened late and rushed off to work...My tears were in the rain drops.

Today you looked so sad—so all alone.... It makes My Heart ache because I understand...My friends let Me down so many times too, but I Love you anyway. Please understand.

Oh,..... If you would only listen to Me...My Love is in the blue Sky and in the quiet green Grass. I whisper it in the Leaves on the Trees, and breathe it in the Colors of the Flowers. I shout it to you in the Mountain streams and give the Birds Love Songs to sing for you.

I Clothe you with warm Sunshine and Perfume the Air with Nature Scents. My Love for you is deeper than the Ocean and bigger than the biggest Want or Need you will ever have in your life. Oh.... if you could only know how much I want to Talk with you and you with Me... We could spend an Eternity together.......Think about it.!

I know how hard it is on this Earth; I really know!.... And I want to Help you.......I want you to meet My Father. He wants to Help you too! My Father is that way you know.

All right,....I won't bother you any further. You are free to choose Me or turn away; Its your decision... I have chosen you, ...you know, and because of this, I will wait....because, I Love you so!

Your Friend,
JESUS

There is a proverb: "As you have made your bed, so you must lie in it," which is simply a lie. If I have made my bed uncomfortable, Please God, Help me to make it right.

author unknown

HEALING 1-10-07

Went for a healing and received the power of God flowing through my back and through my whole inner being. All the back pain is gone and I thank God for my healing and continue to thank him

SPIRITUALITY EXPRESSIONS 1-15-07

Learned much about other denominations. How their beliefs differ from ours and how to speak and pray for them in their faith.

GRIEVING CLASS 1-18-07

Went to grieving class not really knowing what to expect. I learned so much from the mens concept. How they feel and express their feelings about the same issues in life and people around them. Comparing men and womens emotional role. Helping to understand each others emotions. Why they play the role publicly differently. And why. Could share deep personal feelings openly without criticizing, done in truth.

MY LORD 1-19-07

I feel I am in a holding pattern: waiting: just waiting upon you, lord. I am standing at a door, it is closed tight, but I can see into the other side: what is waiting over there for me. What I will be doing and what I will need to do to receive, before I am released to go out to minister. It is so glorious and so close. I can see it, I can feel it. This side of the door, I feel so helpless, so insecure so unsure, so restless. I cannot seem to concentrate and stay with anything. I space out, I pace the floor, I walk with no purpose. I get upset, I get angry. Easily, sometimes for no apparent reason. My patience have gone somewhere else. I need your help, especially with my patience and long suffering.

My dear child: yes, you are in a rest time. What you see on the other side of the door will come to pass, soon, very soon. Those things will be glorious and totally of me. I have shown you only a small part. I have much more to give to you.

You will feel peace: peace beyond understanding. You will be focused completely upon me. I will give you direction, you will not stray or fumble your steps will be sure and steady. You will not feel insecure. I will send someone to come alongside of you. You will grow, learn and serve me as one.

MY DEAR CHILD: 1-29-07

We stand at the garden gate: it is open and weathered. We don't go in the garden we just stand at the open gate and look in. No life, no joy, all the beautiful flower heads, all drooped. Everything is wilted: waiting to be revived. No water flowing ove rthe fountain. Quiet, everywhere is quiet and still. No birds singing. Just flying aimlessly as though no place to l ight: waiting, waiting for revival

You are like a rose bud: tightly entombed, waiting to be nurtured so you will blossom in fullness. You will soon begin to unwrap and shed

your covering and unfold to open to a beautiful sweet fragrance for all
to see your beauty and desire your presence

overflowing oil 2-4-07

Communion with prayer (joyce b). The anointing was so powerful her
hands oozed with abundance of oil and dripping off her fingers. God
was overflowing the anointed oil through her hands for us. You could
feel the oil flowing out of her hand as she laid her hands on yours. I
had the oil pretty well rubbed into my skin by the time I returned to
my seat some time later. When I sat down, my hands too then began
to fill the cups with the oil and it began to drip off my fingers. God did
an anointing for me. I felt that some was for my personal healing and it
also was for future ministering for emotional healings for others, I feel
that this is part of the ministering that awaits behind the closed door
for me. But I will have to learn to listen and step out as God leads me
to develop the healing ministry that he wants me to learn to do. I need
to listen, obey by acting to what God is telling me to do, when, who
and how.

IN THE NAME OF JESUS 2-14-07

You are my salvation. You are my lord, I praise and worship you. Poetry,
lord I want to be able to minister through poetry. Still with your words
and your message but big poetry. People listen and hear poetry. Why
am I pursuing this? To multiply and perfect the poetry ably, what little
I now have. To your glory. I want to write of your thoughts and not my
simple ways.

---

my child many of your simple, as you call them, are, my thoughts they
just seem simple and immature to you. Many are very worthy and they
come from your heart, from you not things others have planted in your
mind they are pure, and yes, some are simple—but they all have a
moral to them for all ages and all intellect. You see, you already have

this gift. You just need to activate it more and let it grow. You have set it aside too long. Use them more in Sunday school class. Nothing is too simple, they all tell a story. Don't listen to the criticism—listen to your heart for I am in the midst; in those simple words, they all minister to the persons they were intended. This is a new time and new place. I have more and better things ahead for you, they still have their place also.

OH LORD 2-22-07

I feel so left out, so alone and outside, so dead. I want so desperately to be a part of the things you are about to release and bring forth. I want to be used and let it be your will. I know these things in my future is preparing and teaching me for—but what about the now, God? I want to be a part of what's happening, what's coming in the spirit realm. I want to walk in the spirit.

My dear sweet child —I have great plans for you. I will use you in a mighty way. It will be me in you, all will see and know. You are just resting for now. Soon I will impart and anoint you for your mission ahead. Soon, very soon. My power and glory will come in like a fire. My people will be over flowing with my ministries, I have planted in each one. Be ready and watch and wait. Be a willing vessel. Listen, hear and write and be ready to move in my power. There is no service too small or too big that I can't do my work. All I need is a willing vessel, sincere heart. Don't let others tell you what and when to move out. Wait, listen for my voice: as you are doing.

Oh God you have brought me so far. I was so far off base from your will. I thought I was right where I was supposed to be. How wrong my thinking was. I am doing things I never dreamed of doing, and best of all, hearing you talk to me. I could never understand how that could be, before I personally experienced it for myself. I thank you lord for never letting me go. It has been a long hard walk and have so much more to go, yet. I know when a door closes that you open another. I just hope I am hearing you right in my heart and am not leaping into the unknown and beyond my capabilities with these disaster services. But I know in my heart I can be a help for the hurting people in their times of need.

Sometimes lord I just want to crawl inside you and receive everything you have for me. I know we can't handle it all at once, we have to learn a step at a time. I just want to be so much like you. I want to wlak and serve in the spirit of you lord. Well I am rambling on. I hope I am not boring you. ----------------------My child I love these talks we have together from time to time.

BLESSINGS: 2-28-07

I am using you. You are doing a very vital work in your serving others. I also know you are blessed and have a great satisfaction when you accomplish something very needful for another. You step up to the plate and get right into the game for the needs to be played. With no selfish intent, only to accomplish their need. When they are not able to function in that capacity.

SO GOOD: 3-2-07

God you are so good. I wasn't sure about the bible but I went ahead and got it all together and gave I to Etta. Lord everything is always just on time: she was looking to order one with large print. Thank you God: thank you, thank you.

MY DEAR CHILD

I see your heart. I hear your prayers for your husband. I feel your compassion for him. I too weep for his pain, he has not asked for my help yet. ---------Holy spirit I ask you to show him truth. Only you can do that. The enemy is telling him so many lies. Lord forgive him. I ask holy spirit to open the eyes of our children that they may see and understand what is really going on with their dad and look underneath the parent realm and see the real person.

THE LITTLE THINGS

Lord you amaze me so with: Kiristin prayed for some fresh live flowers to put in her vase, something alive instead of plastic ones. I am going to visit her and you have me pick two daffodils just for her. Again I wasn't sure. And yes I stole them from anothers garden (the city library) she was so happy to get them. It cheered her right up.

THANK YOU LORD

Thank you for my healing, forgive me of my impatience. I want it all at once and yesterday. Everything is in your timing. ------------------- I see an outer dark circle of warriors, dressed in full armor & spears drawn. An inner circle: a ring of glowing white, like a bright light.

My husband nude as new born and I are standing in center: in open space. He fades in and out of the picture, as though he is being taken and then let go again: but each time he gets fainter, almost as though he is in and out of consciousness.

The outer circle is evil, harmful, trying to attack, to kill and destroy. The inner circle is a hedge of protection. Angels are guarding and warding off the attackers. Being protected. What??? Death.

he faded out of the picture completely.
the inner circle I heard a voice say "I am the light"
nude—he came into this world pure and will leave in purity.

BEAUTIFUL DAY 3-16-07

It is a sunny beautiful day, Jesus and I are skipping down the path to the garden gate. The gate opens wide automatically as we approach it. We are greeted with large beds of pansies, all colors and sizes, all with happy smiling faces. They follow us as we walk along. They are rejoicing.

The fountain is flowing freely and there are bubbles dancing on the pool water, almost as though it is singing "glory hallelujah, glory to the king God almighty". Flowers are coming from all directions, surround us and the pool. All are singing and rejoicing. Praising and worshipping.

It is just a time of praising and worshipping and giving thanks to God almighty it's a time of renewing and refreshing. I don't see any wild flowers or sunflowers, only domesticated flowers. The little birds are swooping down as though they are directing the choir. Everything is so beautiful and awesome in the presence of God. Just want to stay there forever.

CHURCH 3-23-07

Do not allow your "eyes" to deceive you. Listen to your spirit and allow me to speak to you. Do not panic and rush into selfish desires. Seek my face for truth, for I come to build-up not to tear-down. I come to glorify and not bring the body into shame.----------------------

let us not be led into wilderness as Moses led the Israelites through because of their disobedience…

I cor. chapters 5 & 6 Pslm 26:8 "unclean house"

MY DEAR CHILD: 3-28-07

Yes you are my little girl. I pick you up and carry you many times. You are so precious to me. You come to me as a child and you serve me many ways as a childlike manner. You serve in innocence and purity. I love our walks together they are very enjoyable and so precious. --------------------

My children have I not shown you truth? Yet you continue to look the other way to satisfy your desires and not to look for my presence and my glory. I cannot sanctify your actions

this just came suddenly boiling out with firmness and strength

DANCING RAIN 3-30-07

My child I too feel your pain, no not physical pain: you thank me for that healing all the time. I feel your emotional pain, as you have my compassion and my love for your brothers and sisters in the kingdom. Your emotional pain will soon vanish but your compassion will only grow in me. -------------------------------

We are sitting by the pool and listening to the beautiful music of the fountain as the water falls as rain drops on the water below. They dance with joy, they are all around us, each bubble is a different note. As they burst they play beautiful music as though it is coming from a heavenly choir. The birds are joined together and singing in harmony. The flowers with shining faces of joy dance with the rhythm we sit there together and weep in the presence of the father God almighty. Angels as children are circling above in rhythm of the music.

It is so beautiful, so much love that permeates within the whole body. Pansies, so many pansies, with johny-jump-ups mixed within.

4-1-07

My child I want you to attend church with your husband while your church is in transition. You need to be with him for awhile again. No matter what the reply is from the other great ministries.

That's where I want you to be for a time.
this just came thundering out

MY CHILD 4-2-07

You have so much together and come so far over the years. You truly have become as one. You know each other almost as well as I know you. You crossed over many bridges together and moved many boulders that fell in your paths. You were there to pick each other up when you were down. No not in flowing glory but each in your quiet reserved ways. You were always there for each others needs. The walk was not easy at times and very discouraging but you never gave up. You both held true to your vows to each other. Many fall short but you both were strong and allowed me to guide you through each storm. Through it all: today your strength will overcome any obstacle that comes your way for I am in the midst.

You raised your children as they should go: they will return back to me and serve me.

MY DEAR JESUS 4-11-07

Why am I so depressed. Come hold me, you say I am your little girl. Come hold me as you would a small child. It is so depressing at home, everything is so negative in conversations.

My dear child, I am with you always and you have me in your thoughts and, in your activities. You serve me even in your downtime. Yes it is hard to find joy in the midst of darkness, but you always do. You always think of others: finding some ways to help them or planning ahead for others, gifts. You have always put others first. Everything you do is evolved around others needs. You always have someone pictured in your mind that needs something so you gather and plan for. Though you live and minister in a negative environment. You have inner joy and love beyond understanding. How much more can you love me, faithful servant.

PROPHECY 4-20-07

You are blessed among women. A great anointing will come upon you and it will bring an uproar in your house as the glory will fall upon you. Family will come from afar wanting you to help them and they will want what you have. You will lay hands upon them and send them out to minister to others. Two people will come along side of you for bible study to teach. You have been praying for finances and understanding among other things, they will come to pass soon

AMAZED 4-23-07

I have heard your every prayer. All will soon come to pass. I have perfected and sanctified you as my own. I will use you in a mighty way., Wherever I place you. You will be amazed at the things you do and say, but it will be me working through you. I will teach you and you will begin your new journey now. As you step out I will bring more forth.

Trust, listen and obey. Put out all fear and doubt.

REVELATION

I thank you Jesus for the time together you prepared for Fred and his sister. To talk about their hurts of the past—it was a revealing and time of healing for both of them to confess to each other and their individual parts in childhood situations, it gave them both some peace within and forgiveness. I doubt that either realize that was ordained of you for a time of healing and peace in preparing them to go home to be with you, in peace.

We are standing at the garden gate—looking out over the garden. Everything is fresh, new: new seedlings, young plants growing everywhere, as far as you can see. A few dandelions showing here and there, happily showing their smiling faces. Watch for the tares.

This is a new garden, new ground. These young plants need tender care and nuturing to become strong and mature. They will produce great joy and laughter and peace to many hurting souls. This is your field, ready to be harvested. I give all this to you. It will bring blessing and peace to those who will follow and walk into your garden.

Over there is the spring of living water to drink from and to nourish the plants. The more they drink the bigger the blessings and rewards. So water them well, my child: for the spring shall never run dry. Drink, drink, of the living water: give to all who thirst. This is a new day.

THE CHURCH 4-30-07

My children your time has come for new things. You will be planting seed in new ground. Lives will be changed as I am changing you. This is a new time a new day. You will amaze yourself, as those around you. Some will disbelieve and walk away some will mock you. I am preparing my people for the end times, I am removing the tares. Many are called but few will follow and obey. You are among the chosen, time is very short. My fathers house is ready and waiting. I am perfecting my flock. Many are falling away and church doors are closing: but my church will soon overflow and no man can close that door: so I say listen, trust, and obey. I will use you as never before. Seek my face, pray without ceasing

DEAR JESUS PSYCHIC 5-2-07

For give me lord, somewhere I have failed my children. Your words say if we raise them as they should go, they will come back in their old age. I know you are not a God of lies, I stand on your word says that in the end time that many will fall away even some of the elite will fall to the deception of the devil. You have been showing me the darkness, but I blinded my eyes to it in unbelief: forgive me again. I didn't hold him up before you as I should have therefore he fell. I have failed you and my son.

MY DEAR SWEET CHILD: 5-4-07

You have not failed. He made his own choice. He was weak and the enemy step [unable to read] in and filled a void. He failed to follow through his young teachings and follow my leading. Again his choice. I was always there waiting for him in the wings, he chose not to follow as it was too hard and too strict for his liking. You have shown him the way through your walk. He looked the other way: too religious, he says, too strict, no swaying I have to give up too much I can't walk that tight. It is easier to follow the way of the world.

MY CHILDREN (CHURCH) 7-31-07

I have placed a burden on each of your hearts for this church body. I will open the door and pout each person in their place of serving. I will bring multitudes to receive my words and their healing. My house is a house of prayer to heal the sick and broken hearted. You will see and do miracles as many will be healed and delivered of their burdens, for this is a new day a new time as the day is close at hand. The time is now. Bring unto me your sick and hurting, for I am the lord thy God. I am your healer, be not heavy burdened for my yoke is light. Come my children

MY CHILDREN, MY CHILDREN AUGUST 7, 07

I cry out unto you—come, come before me. Come with all your heart mind and soul. Time is so short. Come my children. I have much work for you to do. There are so many hungry and hurting souls crying out. Do you not see them or care about them? My children, my children, their souls are lost, they wallow in darkness. Let me give you spiritual eyes that you may see as I see. My children, my children, your work is unfinished. Go, go. Go into the fields, they are ready to be harvested. You, yes, you. I am calling unto you to go, go now. I will supply all your needs. Go, harvest the fields now. Be not weary I will give you strength, I will give you courage and the wisdom and knowledge. You will have my words, they are mightier than a sword but heals all brokenness with my peace and love. They too are my children they have just never been led or felt my love. They are lost awaiting to be found and brought into my kingdom

IN GODS TIME 8-22-07

My dear child, weep no more for I am with you. Soon he will be free of all pain and be in my presence. I am the healing God, when the drs give up I will heal and make him whole. Hab. 2:1-4

MESSAGES 8-30-07

Lord the messages I get from you seem to go nowhere at times. The opportunity doesn't always seem to come about to deliver the message to the ones intended. So I see them falling on deaf ears. So what purpose are they. I feel they expect me to give a "word" to the congregation. Lord you have not given me that direction only to write what I hear and see: sometimes to speak directly to an individual, sometimes through conversation or again written. I cannot do what they expect me to.

my child, my child. The purpose is that you listen and hear my voice. The more you write the more I can speak to you and you will and do reveal to those as I lead you. The word is spread by mouth to those who will listen as directed. Spreading the good news. It may be few or it may be many. The more you listen the more I can reveal to you. You do give the words to those I direct it to. So it does not fall on deaf ears. One day the doubters will come to you and ask for a word as some do now

(EASTERN OREGON?) 8-28-07

I see a dark grey cloud, fog like, coming out of the ground off in the distance: flat land, desolate, dry. It is rolling across the ground, slowly about five feet high, spreading in all directions engulfing every thing in its path for mile and miles, leaving a path of destruction and desolate, darkness. People and animals wandering in a daze. Many heard but did not listen or was prepared, those suffer much more than they that were prepared. Everything is dry, very dry, like a desert.

interp; first I thought it was fog, but that wouldn't destroy things. So then I thought water like maybe a flash flood, no everything everywhere was dry, no pools of water anywhere. The devastation was like an earthquake had struck. The after affect covers the entire state, all areas of life style. fog=energy=coming from within earth

MESSAGES 8-30-07

Lord the messages I get from you seem to go nowhere at times. The opportunity doesn't always seem to come about to deliver the message to the ones intended. So I see them falling on deaf ears. So what purpose are they. I feel they epect me to give a "word" to the congregation. Lord you have not given me that direction only to write what I hear and see: sometimes to speak directly to an individual, sometimes through conversation or again written. I cannot do what they expect me to.

my child, my child. The purpose is that you listen and hear my voice. The more you write the more I can speak to you and you will and do reveal to those as I lead you. The word is spread by mouth to those who will listen the more I can reveal to you. You do give the words to those I direct it to. So it does not fall on deaf ears. One day the doubters will come to you and ask for a word as some do now

MY DEAR SWEET CHILD 10-02-07

I have many doors, some great ones and some not so great. I will open many doors for you and you will minister to what ever is behind that door. I will be standing there with you. I am with you always. I am your strength. I will guide and protect you. I will fight your battles that come before you. No harm will come before you. You will meet many challenges before you. You will have the victory over all of them. The hurting will find peace and love and receive their healings. Some doors will be filled with darkness, that too you will have victory over the enemies. The mockers will flee as they see my glory approaching. I will shut the mouths of the blasphemous, for they shall see and hear only me.

MY CHILD 10-03-07

I hear your prayers. Yes, I hear every word. I hear your pleading for your husband. A faithful wife prays and lefts up her household unto me. I bless and reward her and her household

CONFIRMATION 10-23-07

Have no fear for I am with you always. Have no fear of the things that lay ahead or the things to come for I am your strength and hope. Trust in me. I am your present and future. I hold you in my arms. Have no fear of the evil one as evil has no hold of you. I am your protector over all that may come toward you. I will give you peace.

THANK YOU LORD 12-10-07

For your provisions and protection. Yes, physically. Emotionally and spiritually. We couldn't have made it through so peaceable without you. You protected us in all ways. Your hand was holding our hands.

yes I provide and protect my children as any father protects his family. You are a family of the kingdom of God most high

NEW THINGS 12-18-07

I pour down blessings upon you. New things are coming your way. You will see miracles as you have never seen before. Healings and yes people raised from the dead. My people will be used as never before. The strong will become stringer and bold and the wek will be made strong. I will give them super power and faith will become the greatest ever revealed. The unbelieving will faint with fear

DEAR LORD 12-20-07

I feel heaviness and sorrow around me. It's like a heavy cloud but yet it's emptiness. People in distance, milling around and softly talking. It seems to get dimmer each day as the fog thickens. It's like we are in quicksand and slowly sinking. God I know you are there and will reach out and pull us back up and out of this mire.

MY CHILD 12-26-07

I see your loneliness. I am with you. Come let me hold you in my arms. I will send people to be by your side to lift you up and comfort you. You are not alone. Your husband also is very lonely, yes, I know. How do I handle it. I don't know anymore. I know he will show disgust at times, everything seems to come back negative or twisted. How do you converse with that? I know it's the illness talking.

MY DEAR CHILD 2007 (self) 12-26-06

Jesus and I are sitting by the pool in the garden. Very brightly colored flowers are everywhere. They seem to be dancing with joy. Many more are coming down the mountain side, running, singing. We are surrounded with flowers, tall ones, short ones.

Sunflowers are gathering into small groups all around us. Smiling, laughing, rejoicing. I will open new doors. I will fill the rooms with the hungry: hungry to hear my word. You will find peace and joy everywhere you look.

You will get a great following, as they look up to you for guidance. You will give me your whole self. Yo uwill walk and talk in my glory. I will impart new things within you. You will wlak in wonderment. You will witness miracles as lives change. I will guide your steps. I will supply your needs. Keep your focus on me. Do not look right or left but directly upon me. Yes, you are standing at the door to be opened soon, very soon.

The anxiety and anticipation you are sensing is about to be fulfilled. I am you lord and God. Let go and let me that I may work and fulfill your purpose.

The uncertainty, the frustration you sense is learning patience: waiting upon me. It's all in my timing. The more you are in my presence the stronger your anointing will become and the deeper your love will grow in me.

ANSWER TO 2007 (self) 1-2-07

Coming together: small groups socializing, learning, teaching, each other. Sharing fellowship, testimonies. Peaceful time. Jesus is in the midst of. Time of rejoicing, sharing, ministering to each other, listening and praying together.

Great following: people will call upon you to meet and fellowship with you. You will hear new ways. You will help people come closer to me

and to know me, not just about me. As you minister to them you will
see changes happen before your eyes as I do a great work in them.

Prepare yourself by fasting and praying for my will in your life and a
closer walk with me. Do your homework, do your studies, seek and you
shall find. Spend more time with me.

DEAR LORD 1-4-07

The body can't survive with long periods of losing all the body fluids.
Lord that's not even living, to live in that kind of pain and frustration
it is a miserable existence, and not very pleasurable. The physical pain
the diarrhea, the infection, the drs say they can't help. Only you, God,
only you. I put him in your hands totally. God will you do something to
help him. I know your word says it is a sin to (murder) to wish someone
death. But God your word also says to be absent from the body is to be
present with the lord. He would be healed and totally free of all pain. I
ask you to forgive me for my thoughts but to look unto my heart

---

My dear child I see your brokenness. I also see your husband broken
body. Yes soon I will heal his body, soul and mind completely. Soon I
will call him home unto me and then I will heal your brokenness and
your life will go on unto me in fullness.

3-4-08

TYPICAL CHURCH

There are leaders, followes, doers and watchers. Some seem to be
involved in everything and know everything.

There are those who are front line people: want to be seen and heard.
Some just want everything that might come along. Some are sincere
while others just take it in: get first and the best.

Then there are the middle few people: sort of laid back but ready and willing if they are called upon to do something as they are willing to be servants. Some will do anything directed their way while others are highly skilled and gifted: they get the job done. Then there are the back pews: don't call me, I can't do anything. I'm too busy don't have time there are plenty other people to do the job. I see some don't do anything so why should I do it all.

Then there are the back of the room people. Some seem to just sit and visit. There are the quiet meek ones. The watchman. The intercessors. The behind the scenes or behind the door people. No one knows what they really do if anything. No glory. No boasting, no fame: they are just there: watching, listening, waiting.

There are leaders, followers, doers and watchers. Some seem to be involved in everything and know everything.

BY THE RIVER SIDE 3-12-08

I sit by the river side in the peace and tranquility. A soft roar of the waves as [unable to read] rush to shore. The river waters are calm, the ducks and seagulls bog up and down and seem to float away with the moving of the water as the tides take them.

The waves splash and break against the old piles. Some seem to glide by with ease and come together again on the other side. Some seem to push and fight their way across, some break up and fall away. God says that is how we are: we are either with him or pushing away from him doing it out way some of us live in peace and look to God for guidance. And things seem to go smoothly as we trust and follow our divine father. While others go with the flow wherever they may lead. They push and struggle in their daily lives. They have never learned to trust and seek the better ways. They aren't ready to give it all to God yet. You can't go part way. You will crash as the waves that broke apart in the passing through to reach the shore: their destiny.

We can learn many things just by sitting at the rivers edge. God can teach and show us many things if we will just sit—wait—and listen as he will speak to us. Be ready to receive what ever he may tell you. He is always waiting and ready to visit with you. He speaks to us in so many different ways. We just have to be ready and willing to sit, wait, and listen

FORGIVE ME LORD 3-20-08

When the ethiopian young man was coming to our church he would thrash and cry out during worship time. Some would laugh at him and others would pray over him and most would stand back and watch. They all said this was the holy spirit at work in him and that is how they do in worship time to just ignore it. But God you showed me that was not the holy spirit, it was demonic. As he loves the lord God almighty and he was possesed by satan and satan was showing his anger through this young man when he tried to worship the true God. You showed me in my spirit yet I stood by and did nothing. I just watched in silence. I didn't even pray against this demonic action. Openly.

God I am so ashamed. Please forgive me. This poor youngman was fighting and calling out for help as he does love you and the enemy was fighting and tormenting him.

The pastor passed this action off as his is the way the ethiopians and people worship. So people stood away and laughed as he thrashed

I am showing you this again as you will see these things again and again as my coming draws nearer. I am preparing you with this knowledge and wisdom.

thank you lord for bringing this back to my memory. I felt so helpless and really didn't know what I should do. I knew it would not be received well.

MY PEOPLE

I am preparing a people to do my work: to serve in a mighty way in these last days. They will do the same things I did as when I walked among you on earth. Heal the sick and weak: raise the dead: deliver them from demonic beings. You will do mighty miracles as never seen before, in my name.

I am separating the sheep from the goats. My true followers from the fence walkers. You will have to sacrifice self from worldly things as I will require your whole self for the glory of the lord: your body, soul and your spirit. Amen and amen. For the time is now.

PLALMS 29
WEARY CHOSEN 3-26-08

There is so much to be done before it is finished. So few to do the work though many have been called. The few are growing weary while the watchers frolic and look away.

Soon I will call my faithful ones while the watchers stand about and remain watching. They will gnash their teeth and weep while I pour out my blessings and miracles over my people. I will lift their burdens and give them super strength so they shall not be weary. I will give them their desires. Their cup will runneth over. They will walk in my glory for they are the chosen ones

HEART BREAK 3-28-08

As I walk around and look at the things around me: my heart breaks.

The places of business: the stores seem to be over-run with things of mans pleasures. Maybe, just maybe off in a corner there may be something resembling Christianity. Oh yes, there is a little, but what? Most seems to point to the new age: and oh don't forget the witchcraft. Oh yes that surely must be there: that's hot: that's the now thing: that's what draws in the people. Immoral. Suggestive games.

The children: girls – oh you must learn about you fairy godmother, every girl has or needs one of those. The magic of the gnomes, the leprechauns, the fairies, etc. Etc etc. You must have that understanding down pat. Oh yes there is a small section for the girls to play house and baby dolls. Oh speaking of baby dolls can you believe what all they can do? Almost everything a real baby can do.

Boys: monsters, the more gruesome the better, satanic figures. War games: killing: toys and games everywhere you look. Where are the sports? God where are you? You are nowhere to be found in any of the sections even in the adults. Electronic games. You might find a bible game tucked away somewhere if you look long and hard enough. Now lets look at the books and music sections: love: romances: and sex. Yes we must not forget the religious section. There are a few of the most popular books that is talked about a lot, but the witchcraft and satanic, they overrun everything else. Now the music: where is the religious section? Oh I don't know. It doesn't seem to sell so we have very little: but what we do have is the modern rock bands the young people prefer them they don't understand the old style music that's all we carry.

Church: the children – keep them entertained fun places to go, activities. We don't need to teach them how to act in gods house or respect the things of God and other peoples, we just want them here.

Parents: be very friendly to them so they feel welcomed. Preach feel good sermons. We can't tell them truth of the future it would scare them away. What happened to the fire and brimstone preaching? Yes it will scare them right into the arms of Jesus. Isn't that what we are suppose to be doing? Don't put any religious pictures on the wall or any religious scenes up, that is infringing on my person rights, how dare you. Some are just sunday christians, they are free to do what they want the rest of the week as God will forgive them again next sunday.

Young men—with your pants hanging off your hips and dragging under your feet and your shoe laces flying about.

Young women—you that come in cover-alls and sweatpants. Your open mid-drifts and low cut tops. This is shameful to God. We are supposed to look presentable and ready to enter any establishment at any time.

DEAR GOD

You should look your best even if it be clean patched work clothing. If its your best you have no need to be ashamed. God accepts us as we are. How would you dress at your wedding or with your best man, in your life? This is gods house it is holy and you are presenting yourself into his chambers. So look masculine and or feminine family—marriage doesn't seem to much these days. We make our own contracts so we are covered on all bases when we separate. We write our own vows. What's the matter with the ones God wrote? Aren't they good enough or are they much too rigid to live by? Then there are the others don't even bother to get married: they have to see if they are compatible, so they don't bother to go through the actions. God where are you? We have to put you under a bushel basket and hid you away. Please forgive us and have mercy for you children.

MY SWEET CHILD 4-17-08

I have told you many time I have much work for you to do. The work I have chosen I will walk you through. At times it will seem overwhelming, that just means to slow down. All will fall into place. I will send helpers to come alongside. They will share the load. I will direct, guide and order each step and each person in their parts.

Good works does not start from the top, build the foundation on solid rock and it will not fail but multiply in my glory.

WHAT DO YOU SEE, LORD 4-22-08

I see a child of God pure in heart, sincere in every way. Loves me deeply within her heart. Doing my will with all her heart. Hears my voice and obeys my word. Rejoicing in doing for me. Loves her fellow man. Has compassion for the hurting. How do people see me, lord: quiet, reserved. Much love and compassion. A watchful eye and open ears. Looking to lead someone to safety and give them hope and encouragement.

ALL HANDS ON DECK 4-25-08 pm FRI

(Before the eve. Meeting) many will receive healing. Many will hear my voice for the first time as I will show them their destiny. They will be amazed and in unbelief as to what I will show them for their future with me. Many has set on the side lines in dismay and wonderment not knowing where or which direction they are to go. They were choosing to see with blind eyes, some with ignorance of my word.

PREPARING FOR WAR 4-26-08 pm SAT

For the coming of the lord. There will be labor pains as never before: as a woman in labor, throughout the world with tribulations and hardships.

This is a new season, a new beginning. Gods waring soldiers marching to trample a fallen enemy and singing praises unto God over the victory. Weapons of warfare, root canal, spritual warfare, supernatural spiritual powers. (Get on your white horse and enter into battle).

HEALED 4-26-08

As I was getting up off the floor somehow I must have twisted my knee wrong as it went completely out of joint. I couldn't walk, was helped to a chair and many prayers went over my knee for my healing. By evening it was a little sore to put my weight on it: by morning (sun) morning all inner pain and soreness was gone: by evening was feeling fine except for a little discomfort if I turned it or bent it back too far. Even the swelling was almost gone. By monday morn all symptoms were gone it was totally healed.

Praise God thank you lord.

STAND FIRM 5-2-08

You are my child. You are my little girl. I have you under my wings. I have you under my shield. I have your household under y protection. Keep your eyes on me. Keep your trust and faith on me. Man is not your source, I am your lord and master. Fear not as no harm shall come upon you and your household. As you stand firm upon my words. Do not falter or doubt as that is the enemy, he comes to destroy and kill. I come to give you life abundantly. Trust. Trust in me as you have never trusted before as these are very trying times. A time of sorting the sheep from the goats. Only my sheep will survive these times. The shepherds will care for my sheep as I direct them. Psalms 91

FIELD OF SORROWS 5-30-08

Jesus waited and met me at the garden gate. When I walked through the gate I saw a sea of red poppies to my left. These are the blood of the innocent, the untold, of my salvation that have perished. There are thousands daily.

To my right is a field of white lilies. These are the righteous that have perished with my salvation. This area is quite small in comparison.

Far off in the distance is a large area of golden wheat — these are the unreached, the unsaved —waiting. This is an enormous area some are tattered and torn, drooping and sickly. Many crying out —help me!!!!

I have shown you the need: the work yet to be done. Where are my servants? Are they too preoccupied with self to search them out? I will supply your needs, you don't need to concentrate on total self. These are trying times and times of testing your trust and faith in me

red—shed blood, war GOLDEN—nature, harvest, glory WHITE—church of Christ

purity, light, righteousness FLOWERS—glory of man YELLOW—fear, warning

LILY—purity, archangel Gabriel POPPIES—indifference, ignorance, sleep, death

WHEAT—bounty of the earth

HEALED 6-8-08

I went to the altar today before the lord and ask for healing help with my gallbladder problem. God was there as always and pouring out his anointing over all.

As the pastor and elder prayed over me I saw (in the spirit) Jesus kneeled before me: with shoulder length golden brown hair and his face aglow as he blessed and prayed over me (the pastor) on my left was the elder praying and their prayers became almost as music they were so beautiful. The enders hand was on my shoulder which I then saw an angel: I heard the name Gabriel mentioned many times (that was the angel by my side he was large and very strong, no not in physical strength but in power of God (dunamis) power. His prayer became as music singing. They were singing in unison then I felt water: like a sheet of water flowing from top to bottom within me

REPORT TO DUTY 6-17-08

Went back to drs today for all test results: complete clean bill of health! All major organs normal and functioning properly. Even the lesion is smaller...praise God.

HEARING 6-17-08

Lord, sometimes I listen to the wrong voice, when it tells me I am not serving you, but in self only. Then you so graciously show me: how my prison sons have grown and hunger for more of you. You show me through karen how you are using and blessing her and ministering to and through her. She too has come a very long way.

Ok lord, I see your works through me I have changed lives and even though I feel it is so little. You show me the greatness. Thank you lord.

Oh yes lord I thank you for my physical healing. Praise God.

VICTORY 6-16-08

An oversized dump truck made a left turn directly in front of me while driving. As soon as I released the gas and began to tromp on the brake: both my legs went into severe muscle cramps. I could not move. I thought "Jesus I need some help here", as my car was approaching the front wheel of this monster truck fast.

Just as suddenly the muscle cramp left my right leg: as it had come upon me. I was able to stomp on the brake and stopped just inches from that huge front wheel of that truck.

The trucks wheel stood <u>way above</u> the hood of my car height.

Victory!!!! Satan you lost again I had no fear or anxiety, trusted Jesus

OPPRESSION 6-28-08

I see Alice sitting at a table working overseeing some papers. She is in despair and weary over the situation: sees no hope, sees no end. In the name of Jesus I command you satan to take away the oppression and take it back to the pit of hell whence it came. Lord Jesus fill her with peace, peace beyond understanding. Show her the open door for her situation and that she <u>will</u> know it is you. May she feel your presence.

MY DEAR CHILD 7-22-08

I have never left you nor forsaken you. No, you have not drifted away either. You are carrying the burden and not giving them to me. I can and will lighten your load but you must release them all to me, and <u>leave</u> them with me. I am your strength. You have allowed yourself to become weary. I am there for you. I am your strength. Give me your burdens and I will give you peace and joy. I will never give you more than you can carry. Go to a sister or brother and together pray unto me, as two or more are gathered together I am in the midst, and you can move that mountain and walk by the beautiful stream and hear and see my glory around you. We can walk together again in the garden. Yes the peaceful beautiful garden. Come my child, my little girl, take my hand.

THANK YOU LORD 7-23-08

I ask for the fire from a prayer warrior. Her reply was: you have it. You already have it! S-oooo I ask God to turn up the flame. Thank you lord for showing me some of my workings of the past. It does encourage me and give me new hope. Yes I am doing some good, ever so small and subtle. How many lord, have I influenced unknowingly? How many seeds have I planted along the way, how many took root, how many fell away untouched? How many time have I missed the opportunity? How many times have I held back and you had to give the task to another? Open my spiritual eyes that I see the things that you want me to see.

Turn up the flame that I may hear and obey. Give me the boldness, your boldness to step out. I want to be used as you call me. I want to do your will. I want to be pleasing to your eye

SO LONELY 7-30-08

My dear sweet child you are never alone. I am there with you always. You are my little girl. I will never leave you. I have people around you praying for you and lifting you up. You just don't see or hear them. They lift you up to me daily. I have a hedge of protection around you, because you serve many needing people. I have a covering over you people come to you, bring their burdens, but you come to me with yours as you feel you have no one else to come to. I am always there to carry you through and lift your heavy heart. I send someone to be your ear, but you hold back. You allow pride and shame to enter in. They too have been where you are. They can give you peace.

Then the enemy comes in with his time clock and closes the door. So you are still carrying your burdens and of those whom you serve.

Alow me to open the door and give you your peace and inner joy.

They too see your brokenness.

TREES (night dream) 8-13-08

I saw a large group of trees (deciduous). Weeping willow (very large tree) predominant. All the tree leaves were covered with dew drops— as a mist. All same color green. Taller trees in the background were oaks, maples, elms, but three stood out most.

when I saw the willow tree I saw waiting, weeping souls. crying out, hurting, broken souls. moving within the branches as though they were lost.

TREES—fluency in revelatory; speech and nourishment; resting place of dead souls. believers and sinners

LARGE LEAVES—powerful; human power of the kingdom. LEAVES –life; the word. DEW—gods gift; fruitfulness, gods word; remnant of gods people. WILLOW TREE, MAPLE TREE, ELM, TREES—THREE varieties –trinity

DEW DROPS—life, cleaning, giving power, refreshing.

WILLOW TREE—PREDOMINANT, weeping, sorrowful

MAPLE—the large leaves, powerful, human power of the kingdom.

ELM—(terebinth) —spreading broadleaf; shade; adultery. sin.

GREEN—go, color of the prophet, indicative of divine activity, prophetic

MIST—spiritual apparition, revelation and transition, spiritual manifestations

(meanings taken from 'the prophets dictionary' by paula price. phd.)

CONSUMING FIRE 8-14-08

God is bringing down a consuming fire upon his people. Watch—be ready to receive, be ready to act upon – the consuming fire will soon fall upon the church. All those ready to receive will receive.

God will pour out upon his people as he did from the mountain top for the Israelites. Wait –watch—be ready for these coming months.

You will be imparted with awesome giftings: supernatural healing, super-natural miracles. Are you ready to receive what God has for you these coming days. Are you ready to act upon. Ask not what you can do but ask God to do what he wants to do through you.

The consuming fire will fall in the churches on those who are ready and waiting. Come, come holy spirit with your fire.

You will see super natural miracles with your open natural eyes manifest in your congregation. I will give boldness to the meek where there was none. I will speak through the quiet ones to all who will be ready and receive my fire.

Wait—listen — (be ready!!!! It is coming very soon upon my church. Your services will be disrupted with signs and wonders. Are you ready. Wait—watch— and receive the consuming fire is coming soon.

HEB. 12:25-29

RELATIONSHIP 8-15-08

We are walking down the beautiful path lined with roses of all colors and varieties, each with its own heavenly fragrance: to the pool in the garden. We are standing by the pool. The water is beautiful deep blue. The water is falling from the fountain gently and softly into the pool below. Some of the droplets are dancing on top of the water while others fall and ripple across the water as waves of glory.

There is a big flock of song birds hovering over head, singing, singing as angels singing unto the lord. Surrounding the pool is a big circle: a mass of sunflowers, all pointed to us and joining in singing along with the birds. They are singing so softly, praising and worshipping. I layed at his feet in his presence, angels hovering over and around us praising and worshipping the lord. Chanting, singing, peace be with you, peace unto God, the almighty God, lord and master.

Holy, holy is the lord God almighty. Holy, holy is the lord

HIS VOICE SPEAKS 8-19-08

Lord I keep hearing you tell me to talk with Margaret H. Of salvation. Lord she has made I clear from day on she was not a Christian and wanted no part of it and didn't want to hear any more sermons as to how bad she is. So I have no idea how to aproach this with her and yes I have given it a lot of thought. So if you want me to do this <u>you</u> will have to give me the words to open the door. I have been very careful not to offend her but yet that she will see you in me and that she <u>will</u> <u>want</u> you in her life. Am trying to be the best Christian I know how to be.

My dear sweet child; you have shown her what a real Christian is—and she is amazed and sees that you are different but don't understand how or why. She has complete trust in you and because you don't preach to her she is comfortable and open with you but still looks down on those who brag "I am a Christian".

Have no concern as to what or how to open the door as I will speak forth the words and give you the knowledge and wisdom to carry on. you will not flinch or show dismay in any thing she will tell you. you will hear with total discernment, you will have total control over your emotion as she unveils her inner self to you. you will not judge her or give your opinions. you will be my ears then you will take this to My Father in heaven and prayer for her salvation.

OH MY LORD GOD 8-20-08

I did as you ask and as you opened the door I was awed at the things I was hearing coming out of her mouth. Yes I did listen intently and sincerely to her: and yes she felt comfortable telling me her deep secrets. I was amazed how you opened the door. I hadn't used that phrase before. "How did you feel or was thinking when you knew you were dying?" And the quesitons you continued to ask as the conversation went on. I gave her name to prayer warriors for her salvation as you said. You are an awesome God. Thank you lord. I have heard of demonic and witchcraft sects but hadn't heard of this one before.

(ROSICRUCIANISM —THEOSOPHICAL SOCIETY)

She would make pentagrams on her floor and go through the rituals. She had the incense and candles. Said that when she would come to the word christian (every time) a rock wall would fall in front of her and stop her from finishing the prayer. She was still doing these things last year 2007

MY DEAR CHILDREN 9-24-08

These coming days: very soon: I shall pour out my spirit upon all my servants: my kingdom will glorify my father in heaven and will glorify my people as they fall of my presence from church to church. As my glory falls within, some will faint as my presence will come overcome them while others will shout and dance with my joy. Soon my children, very soon. There shall be no church services as you know it today. As my spirit shall fall there shall be instant miracles: unexplainable to the untrained eyes. My presence shall overcome every person in the building even those that don't know or serve me. This day is upon you, be ready and watch, as the watchman. Watch, wait and see with opened eyes and rededicated hearts. I will come into the churches and synagogues first and your presence filled with my glory shall fall upon all those you minister too. They too will be my servants. Slave servants: no!. My children of the most high God, the father in heaven. Lord and master of all the universe.

Every knee shall bow and every eye shall weep as they see my presence. You will heal bodies and souls. Pains and afflictions shall vanish before your eyes.

Prison doors will remain unlocked for the glory. The righteous will wander the halls and minister to the guards and personnel and to them with ears to hear the words of the lord God almighty. Songs and shouts shall ring through the halls and echo into the hearts for all to hear. Men will fall upon their knees and cry out in repentance. Lord! Lord! Forgive me!

I feel like Jesus is going to jump right out of me and start doing miracles all around me. strange huh? he is showing me that He is in me and all I have to do is step out in faith and he will do the rest. fear not for I am with you always. it has already been given to me.

testimony
DEAR GOD W.O.P. RETREAT (seaside or.) 10-20-08

Thank you lord for you word. Thank you for your teachings. Forgive me for my ignorance of doing and saying your words wrong. Lord these things I heard all my christian life also the way we were taught it. Not knowing they were wrong, so lord I ask you to help me to correct my ways and remember to say and do it your way. May I hear your voice and heed to your leading and not continue of the ways of my past, especially in my ministering to others. Change my attitudes, give me your ways, your mind set.

Thank you for my healing. I was disappointed that I hadn't received it while the w.O.P meetings were in session. But God you are never late. You are always just on time. The morning service was awesome the teachings and your healing ministering at the end. I'm not sure just what all you did as of yet but I know it was good. When you touched me with your finger I felt the lightning bolt go straight and deep within me then throughout my entire body. Yes it was an electricity bolt. Wow!!! I knew without a doubt that it was truly you and you alone. It was your healing touch you didn't forget. I declare it done and receive it done in your holy name, Jesus Christ of Nazareth

MY DEAR CHILD 10-23-08

Yes I have set your destiny before you were born. I knew every torment and stumbling stone that lay ahead in you walk of life. I know your downfalls and weakness. I have taken you in my arms and carried you many miles. There has been many walls put before you but you always managed to break through them. I have given you strength when and where you have needed it your walk has not been easy but you have made it. You have come a very long way. I am now opening new doors for you, some will be difficult but I will walk with you: others will be joyful, I will be there also. I have given you much wisdom. You have trained yourself with much knowledge. Now is a new season and a new day, to put all of that together and use it for my glory. You are my chosen child as you have come and served me, as my child

BLACK DAY IN HISTORY 12-18-08

I see a very large dust cloud rolling toward me. As it approaches it grows bigger and gets darker and speeds up. The bigger it gets the darker it gets and becomes very black. Seems to cover and engulf every thing in its path, especially people and big buildings. People are crying, tumbling and screaming. I can see an overlay in very big print: the number 20. I see this as a dark time coming in history for the U.S.A. Will also involve some other nations. It feels very frightening in my spirit. With dramatic effects on the entire nation. All phases of and levels of government will be in turmoil. All levels of departments in complete chaos without direction or leadership.

Will deepen hardships and break apart families and corporations and cause martial law. Dark days lay ahead for our nation. People will have to totally trust in God to survive this time until new national leadership is put together. But there will be unrest and distrust at all government levels. It will bring the churches into unity.

It will deepen the distance between the nationalities in our nation and more distrust from the nations of the world.

The war between Israel and Giza, and Palestine: I believe this is the bringing together (unity) of the world to openly bring fault against Israel. The world, countries, will be in agreement and now can bring their their governments together in the final plans in warfare to bring Israel down. But God is with Israel. Israel will stand.

The church (religion) will take on a new form.

HE SHOWED ME THE TREES

While I was walking through the trees talking and Praising Him,
He showed me the trees. He said, "look up into my forest.
See the trees which stand tall and stately, gently swaying in my
gentle winds. These trees are as you are, I will show you.
Look up into the tops, the tall straight ones. That is how you
are when you are walking in Me, and you are mature in your
Christian walk. The fuller the tops of the trees the more you are
serving Me.
The broken tops are the backsliders. They stumbled and fell, and
in their self-pride they didn't think to ask my help. No-one
came along and helped them back on their feet so they gave up
and live the best they knew how, they only came to My house for
special occasions, My Birthday and my resurrection. Maybe if
someone would come along and ask them to attend once in a while
they would come visit me. They "knew about Me" but never "got to Know
Me". But they are born again and still in My kingdom.
The deformed and bent-over ones, they too are My children.
But their walk was full of trials, tribulations. They suffered much,
as they tried to walk it on their own. But someone saw their broke-
ness and gave them My hand. They were lifted back up into hope
as they were delivered of their sicknesses. They are walking
strong and cry My name when the stumble. I guide them down the
straight and narrow again. See how straight and into the light
the top goes now.
Now you see the dead trees with a sadness in your heart.
They are the ones who are dead in sin. They closed the door and
sealed it. wouldn't let me in.

Now look ahead and see the ones over there the ones with their
green gowns down to the floor. They were dedicated to Me while in
their mothers womb, and grew with my grace and glory in My Fathers
house. Those I have set aside to be the Shepherds to disciple My
sheep.
Then He said, look again, look all around, into My beautiful Forest;

what do you see? What do all these trees have in common?
Yes my child, the dead and broken limbs. Not one was left untouched.
Notice how much more some have than others. It took some longer
to hear My voice. They tried to do it on their own and failed, before
they learned to trust and obey, Me.
Lord, what kind of tree am I? How do you see me?

MY CHILDREN CHURCH 1-05-2009

This is a new beginning, a new season, a new day. Old things shall pass
away as I bring new things into your church. I will bring together the
believers, servers and the doubters. Every believer will have a place of
service in my kingdom, from the young to the very old.

I shall move in a new and mighty way within the body. The weak and
the doubters, the manipulators and the lazy. Yes, each one shall be
awakened and shall be moved.

Services will not be the same as I move in and around and touch
individual some will shout, some will weep and moan, some will fall on
their faces in repentance. They will speak in many tongues while some
will fall and lay under my power and arise with revelations.

There will be no time set. As my time is not your time.

Many seekers will come to receive and be a part of my moving while
some will come only to observe but will fall away quickly in unbelief.
These things will be the new season, the new beginning. Be ready, wait
and watch.

A GARDEN WALK 1-15-09

As we walked and entered in the garden there was a stillness. The
sunflowers all had their heads bowed down. They were encircled in
rows looking to the ground. Yellow flower petals were falling from the
flowers onto the ground for a fallen sparrow.

When I saw the sparrow, I fell to the ground, sobbing uncontrollably. Jesus bent down and picked up the little sparrow and put it in my hand and said: this small one fell with a broken wing but with prayer: someone came to its aid and picked t up and helped it heal its brokenness as I will mend your brokenness.

As I led you to this broken spirit, I will bring someone to your side. Many flocks of small birds are flying and singing overhead with joyfulness. The sunflowers heads are all pointed up to the sky and nodding as though to say: thank you for retrieving this little tiny soul. God cares for every living thing.

He stands waiting with open arms for us to call to him and the angels dance and rejoice.

Lord I humble myself, I bring yself in my nakedness before you.

for your cleansing healing of my brokenness. I am like that small sparrow with a broken wing.

THE BODY OF CHRIST 1-23-09

If my children will worship me in truth and spirit, I will pour out my blessings: so many you cannot contain them all.
My glory will about. You will see with spiritual eyes and hear with spiritual ears. Freedom, freedom! Freedom!!
Worship me in a free spirit. See what I will do through you.

2-11-09

PRAYER—DECLARE HIS GLORY

Glory, glory, unto God almighty lord of heaven and earth.
Glorify his name above all the earth. Declare his glory!
Great is the lord master, <u>worth</u> of praise. Worship the lord in
Splendor of his holiness! Ascribe to the lord the glory due his
Name. Let the heaven rejoice and the earth be glad in it.
The lord reigns.
The birds sing his sweet songs and the clouds speak his words.
The lightning lights up the world as the earth sees and trembles.
The fields are jubilant and everything in them. The trees of the
Forest will sing for joy and the mountains melt like wax.
While the heavens proclaim his righteousness and all the people
Declare his glory

psalms 96

THE GLORY REALM 2-11-09
AGLOW

Let my glory fall. Let my glory fall upon each one of you,
May you feel and experience my awesome holiness.
Nothing else can compare, I am with you always but my glory
Awaits for you to prepare to receive it.
Worship me in wholeness that my glory
Shall cover you in completeness

THE BEAUTIFUL GARDEN 3-2-09

As we walk hand in hand through our garden: the garden of love and splendor. We walk through the field of lilies, their whiteness shows the purity and splendor as the father in heaven. Their golden antlers glitter with the glory as it falls upon the petals.

The bed of red roses: the blood of Jesus that was shed by the lamb of God for our healing and salvation, their delicate fragrance of the the lord God fills the air.

What are the purple flowers Jesus? They are the morning glories, the new day. The purple of royalty. Their vines is the trailing of his robe. The velvety glow of the flower is the glowing of the spirit of God. The babbling brook is the freshness and newness. It is the beginning and the ending, the everlasting eternity and the living waters which flow freely through and within each of us for we are the chosen ones. All of these things and much more are in our fathers heavenly mansion.

TESTING TIMES 4-6-09

Lord, I am seeing these times of confusion and turmoil as a growing and testing of our faith, a time of preparation and judgment. The ones that are focused in you and trusting you in these times will be watched over and you will supply our needs as your word says.

Those trusting in man and the system will plunder and fall for these times are the prewarning and testing of the things to come. The lion will devour the weak and unfaithful while the angels of the lord are guiding and protecting the kingdom of God. As harder times are coming, as poverty and famine continue to spread around the world. Your wonderful ways you will take care of your people. You are the lord and master of all things, and these things must come to pass before you can return to earth. Many will lose hope and fall away from the kingdom, while others will come running into your arms. We are at a time of self testing of who is our lord and master. We must trust and believe with all our strength in our lord God almighty. You are God, the one and only.

HOW DO <u>YOU</u> SEE? 4-7-09

Jesus is waiting by the gate into the garden. The gate is covered with rambling vines and thorny bushes. Jesus speaks to them and they part and let us through only to quickly close behind us. To our <u>right</u> <u>is</u> a beautiful field of all kinds and colors of flowers with many colorful birds, and animals grazing and fleeting about. To our <u>left</u> is <u>desolate</u> and famine. Broken down buildings, people living in poverty. Women searching and weeping, searching to find food and shelter for <u>her</u> family

These two scenes are separated by a living babbling stream of clear cold pure water. Children are running and playing in the stream. Laughter abounds. Jesus says: all they need to do is cross over: come to the other side. This is the living water, this side will provide all their needs and I will walk with them through these hard times. I will give them peace, strength, to overcome. I will carry them through these devastation times. A time of hope and faith as long as they put their trust in me and not the world. These who put their faith in me will survive and be strong for the darker days to come.

As you have filled my storehouse, you now have plenty. Keep your eyes on me and obey my commands and your blessings shall be many. Follow me, I am the way, the alpha and the omega.

I brought you here to see the world as it is today. The many of the world and the few of the kingdom. These things are warnings of things worse to come. Many have blinded eyes, my chosen see with my eyes into the future which I have told them. They have faith and trust in me and not the things of the world that fall and burn

testimony
phone call 4-9-09

Received call from dr when I arrived home: to make appointment about my mammogram test. We need to make a decision about more testing as the xray was not favorable. Well I panicked. I was devastated, terrified.

Started praying to God and asking for a word, any word.

After awhile I started to get two words: cystic fibrosis: over and over. I am with you always. Have no fear as fear is not of me. I will give you peace and strength and you will give me the glory. The following Sunday at church I received some awesome prayer from the aglow ladies. I now have peace about it.

A NEW BEGINNING: PLANTING SEED 4-9-09

We are walking through the garden its like a spring day after a refreshing spring rain everything is fresh. Washed and bathed with the warm sun. The rains have nourished the earth and new growth: new beginning, comes forth everywhere. A new life, a fresh start. Old things and old ways will fall at the wayside and new things, new life, new beginning takes it place new doors open for the new life as the old ways are taken away, new ways new life styles: are you ready for the change??

These new plants and new gardens will flourish and grow and produce as never before. It is a new beginning a new life. Notice the gardens are small to begin with, but new seed will be planted daily and the gardens will multiply a new harvest will grow daily. The more seed you plant the bigger the harvest the work is easy. Just walk through and water with the living water.

My glory shall shine from my father above. Are you ready my child?

I will supply the water you need to supply the seed.

This is what I have waiting for you and my church

TELL MY PEOPLE 4-21-09

I see dark, very black clouds forming, off in the distant sky. As they come together they are slowly moving toward and over the United States. We will be overcome by this darkness, and will pass throughout the world. Tell my people not to fear for these things must come to pass, for these are the last days. These are the alpha and omega.

The one who you have put high on a pedestal, and the world adorns, will lead you into these darkened days.

Tell my people to watch and be ready: search for I am in the midst, seek my refuge for I am your strength. Search my words for I have given you warnings, for many are ignorant. Tell my people to wait, listen and watch. Be ready for these days are coming soon. Open the blinded eyes and the deafened ears. You are my stewards

vision 4-26-09

A dream in the night. I was standing beside myself watching the dr as he moved over my body with the x-ray wand, three times. Each time he said "I can't find it: 2-I can't find it 3-I can't find it. And told me to go home. I take this as a word from God. I will claim it and stand on it.

SEEK MY FACE 4-29-09

Pray as you have never prayed before. Be on your face before your God, for he and he alone will give you the strength and faith you will need through these coming days. For as the skies darken so will lives strive for survival. But you who seek my face, I will guide and protect. I will be your strength and provider, I will be your guide and protector!

Do not look to man for he shall deceive you. I am the way and the truth. I am your strength. I am the alpha and omega.

total peace 5-7-09

This is the day. I have total peace. Yes I have anxiety of the needles, but God will give me the strength to endure that too. Its all in Gods hands. I believe. I give God all the praise and glory and I am claiming the victory

drs office 5-7-09

Saw dr. Did all the preliminaries. The ultra-sound shows it loud and clear duplicate of the first pictures. Dr marks out detail and reexamines to prepare for biopsy procedure. Checks and rechecks with pictures and reexamines. Takes previous pictures and present pictures and compare them finding them exactly the same. Sits on chair puzzled. They are the same: I cannot find anything in the breast. I don't understand what is not working together here something has taken place I don't understand. I told him again that God was in charge and he took care of it. He shook his head and said "I agree with you. I would hate to think that I missed it and something bad shows up later. I will send all of this on to Portland for further evaluation and I will do what ever they say." I declared the healing praised and thanked God. On the way to the hospital for the test my husband said: why are we doing this as this is a wasted trip there isn't anything wrong. That was confirmation.

What I failed to realize at that time was when the dr could not find it and I was showing on the x-ray screen. God was saying see I told you there was nothing to be concerned about and your not listening wow!!!

THE STORM 6-12-09

My dear child: I am taking you through the storms. You will stand strong and firm. The mighty winds shall not move you. The waters shall rise but you will rise above them, it shall not overtake you.

The lion shall roar and raise his head louder but you shall receive no harm for your ears will be deafened. Your ground will shake but you are built on solid rock. The storm shall roar and seem to never pass. Through it is just for a season. You are as a tree among many in the forest. You will not bend or break you stand tall in my strength. I see a forest of many trees, some are broken and frayed. One stands above the others, straight and tall with some bent and lower bruised limbs, but they have healed and mended. New ones continually come out and grow, reaching heavenly bound.

VOICE OF GOD 6-12-09

God of glory thunders and
Is powerful and majestic.
Strikes with flashes of lightning.
Twists the oaks and
Breaks in pieces the cedars
Shakes the desert places.
Sits enthroned over the waters,
Enthroned as king.
Blesses his people with peace.
This is the voice of the lord. Psl 29

WAR DRUMS 6-30-09

The war drums are beating louder and longer. The armies are getting restless. The war lords are gnashing their teeth.

Warriors this is no time to sleep. Intercessors be on your faces day and night uplifting the saints. Pray for the weak and unsaved for the angels of the lord are crying mercy, mercy.

The serpent has raised his ugly head. Soon he will spit out his venom and fury.

Tell my people to be ready, be ready!! Be ready, as your victory is at the door

Do not down your eyes to the thing that circles your feet: but set your eyes upon the heavens for the glory of God is nigh

HEED MY WORDS 7-20-09

Oh my children: you must heed my words. So many of you have closed your ears and covered your eyes. You are rejecting my warnings of the coming days. You are mocking my servants and laugh at their sayings. Oh my children these things are now upon you. Many will suffer as they reject my warnings. The prophets of old are the same as of today. Some listened then and some scorned. Beware my children as these days are numbered.

As in the days of Jacob thousands fell and so shall it be in these days of time. I am your strength and way. The I am: the alpha and omega.

JACOB___Israel-supplanter—usurper who displaces. Struggled with man and God. Outwardly brash and grasping but always enriching himself and securing his future. Anointed of Bethel

BE READY 7-30-09

Be ready my children for the hour has come. Stand on solid ground as sinking sands abound for if you are not ready you will be devoured. The serpent has raised his head and the lion roars: and you shall be overcome. Come my children let me cover you with my wings.

WAITING AT THE GATE 7-30-09

Jesus is waiting at the garden gate for my arrival.

His arms stretched out as I approach he is calling "come my child".

We walk through the gate and he takes me and holds me tightly in his arms and says these are the days ahead. (Sorrow)

See the <u>flowers</u> of the <u>fields</u> with all their <u>heads</u> <u>bowed downward</u>. These are my <u>intercessors</u>, prayer <u>warriors</u>. They are lifting up the saints unto me and crying out for the <u>weary</u> and unsaved. My father hears their <u>cries</u> and holding shut the <u>serpents</u> <u>mouth</u> for a short <u>time</u>. This is what my children need to be doing while he prepares your <u>hearts</u>.

As you see in all <u>directions</u>, my children. All <u>nations</u> and all <u>creeds</u> are in <u>mournful</u> prayer

MY DEAR CHILDREN 8-21-09

I hear your prayers, I see your weeping for those you care about.

I am with you always.

I see dried up dead desolate land. The ground is dry and cracked deep. All plant life is dead and broken. This is (famine). There is a big red barn like building way off in the distance, people dressed in white, busy in and out of building. A long line of people dressed in black walking away in opposite directions (the storehouse)

This vastness goes as far as I can see in all directions (the nation) there is a lone brown starving horse searching for food.

This is not caused by lack of rain, this is a supernatural cause.

Those that have laid up treasure in my storehouse, I will supply their needs. My children watch and be ready, this time is upon you

THE ROCK WALL (DREAM – VISION) 10-5-09

I am climbing up a wall, like the wailing wall in Israel. I was rock climbing, with the aid of a rope. The first time I made it all the way to the top and stood up. Came back down the rope and was to climb up again this time I could only go about ¾ of the way up and fell back to the bottom. Tried again and this time only about ½ way and fell back down. Tried the fourth time and couldn't get off the ground only about three feet. There was an angel standing at the top encouraging me but I still couldn't make it back up again. I felt I failed, defeated

letter to Jesus Oct. 8-09

My dear Jesus and holy spirit: I love you so much. I thank you for my salvation. Thank you for teaching me, you show and teach so many things some new, some old, each in its own special way. The garden walks are so very special. Some times I am not sure if I'm really hearing you or is it my wandering mind. Forgive me for my doubting but I so desperately want it to be from you and you alone. I want to hear and see in truth. I want spiritual eyes and ears. I want to sit and sup with you. You have taught me so much through your creations, how can anyone deny your works. I know I don't spend time with you or meditate in your word like I should, I'm sorry lord. I just want to be in your presence and try to obey your word.

MY DEAR CHILD: its ok to have doubts, for Thomas doubted. I would rather you have doubt than to run and believe everything you see and hear. Satan is a master of disguise and he continually kibitz to deceive. Our garden walks are special as you bring sunshine where there may be a weakness. you have such joy and understanding with the plants. I love to see your relationship with my creations, it is a special kind of love. You are my chosen one. I have filled you with my love. xxxxxxxxxxxxxxxxxxxx WISDOM: the word says; come unto me as little children.

I try to come to Jesus with a child like manner. He receives me as a child. He calls me His "little girl"

Jesus doesn't want fancy words. He wants us just as we are; plain, simple. Don't try to portray something you are not.

WANDERING PEOPLE (DREAM-VISION) 10-15-09

I am watching a group of people wandering, walking in a field. No general activity or games or talking, just walking and wandering around as though they are lost and looking for something. Who are these people, dressed in everyday clothing, all ages, men and women. I know all these people, some are very close friends but most are family and relatives, all have passed away, dead.

I am just standing and watching, waiting, to see what or where they are going or will do.

MY DEAR LORD JESUS AND HOLY SPIRIT 11-12-09

I'm so sorry I miss your directions and I don't always obey. I'm not always sure it is you and what you want me to do. I sometimes think it is just my wishing, my thoughts. Please forgive me.

I'm so sorry I still sin against you. My mind thoughts are not always in line with yours. Please forgive me. I'm so sorry if I am so busy doing your work I don't take time to spend with you in your chamber. Help me lord to be with you more and not so much about you. Lord I want so much to please you and be your servant I forget to spend time with you personally to worship and praise you and to talk with you.

I want so much to be more of you, I want people to see you and feel you through me. I need to perfect the fruits of the spirit more and not concentrate on the gifts, as they will manifest in your timing.

Lord I have come so far with you but I have so much more to overcome.

Lord I am asking you to take my hand and walk with me, guide me through the hoops that I may be pleasing to you and you can say "well done my child". Lord I am asking a favor of you to place me and put me where you want me to be and to do.

My hearts desire is still to teach and help the hurting and abused women. Again lord I want those that come along side to be your anointed, with your heart, that this can be your love and compassion reaching out to those needing your touch in their lives. I know you didn't put all those lessons together to set on a shelf. There are souls that need to be reached.

I know my family see you through me, some don't understand it all but I know they desire it. Others don't understand it and are afraid of it. Oh lord open their eyes and soften their hearts that they see and desire and reach out to you.

I need much more help with my patience and condemnation with others, especially with those I am close to

I know I am so immature in so many ways. I still come to you as a little child. I act and I speak as a child but y heart is hungry for you. I can walk ten feet tall as I know you are my lord and savior. You are mine and I am yours, even though many times I feel so faraway and lost. I feel as though I haven't earned my place in the kingdom yet. I know you love me, you have never left me and you gave your all upon the cross at calvary for my salvation, my healing. You gave everything and I have so little to give you back and I seem to manage to mess that up at times.

IN THE GARDEN 11-17-09

Jesus and I are standing in the middle of the garden area, the sky is dark and overcast. The fields are vacant of flowers, its dead winter time: desolate, empty of all life. Paths zigzag throughout in all directions. You can almost feel the joy and laughter as people walked through and enjoyed the beautiful flowers and birds singing. Picked all the flowers they wanted, it was freedom and glory everywhere. Now, it is a time to rest, and prepare for the coming days ahead, yes, there is hope, there is life, there is light ahead. But one must look beyond this time, now. In the east is a very bright beautiful ranbow. Yes, the glory of God saying: I am here, I am the hope, the now, the future. Do not fear of the dark days ahead for a new light shall sooon come again. A new life shall abound as all this desolate harshness will soon pass away.

The storms must come for behind every dark cloud there is light with new life.

LETTER PRAYER 12-29-09

Dear lord Jesus

Please forgive me for being so unthoughtful. You have given me so many blessings and multitudes, that I have no knowledge of.

I have a wonderful family and a wonderful church family of the kingdom of God, the father in heaven. What more could I ever want more of.

Thank you my lord

I hope I haven't burdened you with my babblings. Next time I come into your chamber I hope to be more cheerful and more respectful of your reverence. In my limited vocabulary I have no words that I can describe you adequately.

my dear little girl; I have given you much wisdom and knowledge through your years. when you were very young you had much wisdom and knowledge beyond your years. and today you use them very wisely and always to the right time and place. I am your father in heaven and I love for you to come into my chamber and tell me all your thoughts. I made you and I have always looked over you and guided you though your life.

You came to me as a little child, even before you knew about me or who I was. I was your imaginary friend, you always talked to me when you were frightened alone, locked up in that dark smelly place. You were so precious and innocent, you are still my little girl. I always came when you called and you always knew I was there with you. You still call my name and talk with me in your troubled times, you still sit on my lap, I still told you in my arms, you still are my little girl.

When you ask me to come and be your lord and savior the angels in heaven sang and danced and I wept with joy. psl. 91:14-16

MY CHILD 3-17-10

You stand at the door, waiting with open arms, waiting to see who comes through that needs your helping hand. What is their need today? A word to lift their spirit, a small gift, to bring them joy and peace. You have so much to give them. They only need to ask and be ready to receive it. You take them by the hand and guide their way. You give beyond their spoken needs. You see within and hear their inner voice. You bring them into my presence though some fail to receive my glory, but the seed does not fall on rocky ground to be washed away. You serve me in a mighty way.

A WALK IN THE GARDEN 3-18-10

It is a warm spring day. The roses at the garden gate are budding with new growth. Yes, it is a new season. Small flowers, tiny flowers. Flowers of all colors and types everywhere you look.

New growth: born again, these are like a new Christian, born again, awaiting to be nurtured with love, warmth, tenderness. Some just emerging as coming out of a cocoon, to flourish and mature into a beautiful glowing flower. This is what I do for each new child into my kingdom the brook is flowing full, cleansing and washing away winters debris. The water flows and rushes, purifying everything in its path. My dear as you gaze upon this you see this as a new season, new life, creation and beauty. I see it as my kingdom. Everlasting. The living glory of my father in heaven which is well pleased. And my child you are a part of all of this for every one you bring into my kingdom in heaven, you are planting a new flower in the garden of eden. Each one different than all the others. As you are different of any other.

Look upon the tulips, all dressed in many colors, dancing in the breeze. Daffodils with their shiny faces and their bells ringing as they call out, come my children lets sing praises and worship unto our lord! The lilies tall and elegant as guards at the door spreading their fragrance and the winds scattering their glory (pollen and fragrance) across the lands. The butterflies dressed in their finest and the birds singing as angels of above. This my dear is the fields ready for harvest.

Thank you Jesus for pointing out to me that these walks in the garden are you taking me into your chamber. for we walk, talk share, weep and just sit quietly in each others presence

GARDEN WALK (vision) 4-6-10

As we walked through the garden gate, the beauty, the fragrance and the peace. The heavenly music, overwhelmed us, its so glorious I fall to my knees and weep as Gods presence overcomes me. Angels dancing and singing. Even the flowers seem to be dancing and glowing as flames, dancing, everywhere you looked.

Then Jesus said: this is but a small glimpse of what awaits my children, at which I now am standing at the door, waiting for my fathers call: calling his children home. My child the hour is so near.

Then he took my hand, and we walked a short distance and suddenly, there was devastation everywhere. There was nothing recognizable. Everything was broken, destroyed, blackened. Fires were everywhere. People screaming and running with torment, trying to escape and find some peace.

Then Jesus said: my child I cannot show you any more as it is much to horrible. For these times, too, are at the door.

My children need to be on their faces, praying, repenting, cleansing and preparing themselves to meet their father in heaven

(Envision)

It's a large golden ball of swirling light, but not blinding or difficult to look into it. It seems to glow from within, the light swirls <u>swiftly</u>, but it's transparent. You can see everything but yet nothing; cept the glowing, light, ball. But there is man like image (figure) that seems to show through from deep inside. The voice speaks with soft tenderness, and the energy, that flows from the voice, seems to go right through you as though you aren't there: like a wind.

A SPOKEN WORD 4-20-10

Thank you lord for your awesome love. Thank you for your words you bring forth through other sisters. Words that I need to hear both encouraging and fulfilling. I think I heard you say: my joy, your joy, I keep locked up inside, within me. I need to be me, not what others want me to be, to be myself. To be free in speech and actions. That I may be while in you. To step out in boldness and do your will, step out in wholeness. You delivered me on my bondage, as I was held captive. I know I have been changed. I am to learn to love myself and not allow to be put down anymore. I know you have and are doing a miracle within me. I feel your inner presence I feel there has been a deliverance and feel there has been a healing. And feel a physical healing in process. I feel I am now able to speak out and come against the control that comes against me. I now have freedom. I do feel an inner peace. I know I can do more deeper things for you now when you tell me to step out and go, do. I can in complete faith that you are with every moment. I see you opening new doors, of unknown, new ground. You also told me three or four times I was a virtuous woman. Thank you, I needed to hear that. Thank you for using a sister to deliver your message to me. Psl 116

HEAVENLY GARDENS 4-30-10

We walk together through the garden gate. The gate has an arbor covered with roses, so many you see only flowers, no greenery just a bed of beautiful flowers, no dead or wilted or straggly ones just all perfectly formed flowers. The fragrance is so soft and heavenly but yet so soothing it embraces your every part of your being, yes it is the fragrance of the lord. Everywhere you look is glowing beauty, yes glowing as flickering flames dancing and calling out. You can see the fragrance and the colors intermixing and merging as one yet so individual. You can hear the sounds of the music flowing as a soft wind over the flowers

I can hear the gentle trickling of the water as it flows through and around in the flower beds as refreshing and nourishing the plants. The fountain, yes the fountain off in the distance, stands high above everything around it. The water falling gently from the top, which looks a very large jar, or jug. The water flows so softly and gently and seems to appear as if it come out of the rock itself. It is crystal clear one can look deep into the pool and see the bottom. It is so clear and pure. Drink mychild for this is everlasting eternal life I give to you. All of this my child is my love, my blessings:

I give to you freely.

(PRAYER) TO OUR NATION (USA) 5-6-10

We humble and repent before the lord God almighty.
We hide our face before him with trembling
For we have disgraced, disobeyed and unfaithful.
Therefore we have become as a disease a canker,
As we intermarried with leaders of other gods.
We are filled with pollution by corruption,
Of the people with our evil deeds
And selfishness with great guilt
Our sins are higher than our heads,

And our guilt has reached the heavens.
Because of all this, none of us
Can stand straight before you, lord
Our day of judgment is upon us,
For the moment, the lord our God, has been gracious

based on Ezra 9

FRESH CLEAR WATER 6-7-10

As we walk through the garden one can feel pain and sorrow everywhere. There are many broken flowers, some are laying flat on the ground, other [unable to read] are bent over, some with broken flower petals fallen to the ground. So many broken bodies. Some whole families (one variety or area). My child go to the spring and fill your cup with fresh clear water, and take it to all the broken and hurting, for these are many of my people hurting and broken bodies. Many have broken spirits, go to them, take a drink of my healing water to them. Go to the families first for the healed families will bring blessings to those around them.

One by one you shall bring them unto me and they will be made whole. As we walked through the flower beds they began to rise up like jumping-jacks, popping up all around us. This my child I smany of my people today, but their healing is drawing near as they reach out and you step out with your fresh clear water answering their call, they will be made whole again. Come my child, there is much work to be done, we will walk together

WALKING TOGETHER 6-24-10

As I approach the garden gate I see someone else standing, waiting for me. I walk through the gate, behold there stood my husband also. Jesus takes us through rows and pathways, through the forest of many different kinds of flowers. First were the small belly flowers (ground cover types) this is where you were when you first married. Then through the spring flowers, the tulips, daffodils, crocus. Full of joy and laughter, children playing. The world is at your feet. The next group were the summer flowers, all kinds. Brilliant colors, fragrance fills the air. But with a closer look there are some weeds and even some heavy ones with great thorns mixed in. Those are the years of turmoil and pain. Only one of you knew me and sought my face. These hardships were deep seated, some seemed to never end. Life became very difficult, but I never left you, I was there always for the asking. One day, Fred faced life and death and reached out for your salvation and your life made a complete turnaround. The angels in heaven danced and rejoiced as did your wife after many long years of praying for your behalf. I was then able to pour down my blessings. Both of you then turned to me for all your needs. Now we look around and can see the entire field of all the flowers, the weeds are almost gone and the thorns have withered and died. Now you walk together as one with all my blessings. You both have come a very long way. Yes, there are still stumbling blocks in the pathway, but together you will conquer and have the victory over all. All this beauty that surrounds you will clothe you for the world to see and envy as your lives pass by you are so loved in the kingdom of my father God. You are my children, you are my chose ones.

THE CROOKED BRANCHES 7-9-10

We approached the garden gate, there were rambling vines everywhere, choking and entangling everything in its path. The beautiful roses can barely be seen. As you look across the fields of what was beautiful colorful flowers are now gone, just an occasional bloom can be visible the path-ways are rocky and very difficult to manage. There are weeds and briars, vines of all kinds smothering the plants. One can barely find any plants that one can recognize. The flowers are tattered and torn, struggling to come through the maze to survive.

These are the times, my people are struggling, some are overcome completely. You must keep your eyes upon me at all times or you will be devoured. You must sincerely pray for my intervention as these times will worsen as these branches gather their strength. You must warfare to take out these poisoned weeds or they will overtake. For my people are being smothered and consumed by this poison. I will never leave or deceive you. You must interceed for your nations, I will give you strength to overcome. These branches will consume the world. I will give my people strength, hope, and peace. I am with you always

TROUBLED WATERS 8-2-10

Jesus meets me at the garden gate. There is such peace and tranquility as we walk together. Beauty and the fragrance surrounds us. Birds are singing from the tree tops. Wrens and sparrows race across the pathway ahead of us as though greeting us. One can hear their little chirps as they talk to each other. We slowly walk over to the fountain and sit by the water. Watching and listening as it softly falls into the pool below. A gentle breeze comes through and troubles the water and it then again became calm and peacefull as the winds blow by. He takes my hand and gently says "the troubled water from the winds that came through is like the troubled time that lays ahead for you. It will be a short but troublesome. As the season calms, you will again be in complete peace. I will send people to come around you to lift you up. I will be at your side walking with you as I am now sitting here with you. Keep your eyes and ears forward upon me at all times. The peace and serenity you feel today will return and be with you always. All you need to do is come and I will fill you cup with my clear water

MY DEAR CHILD 8-17-10

Yes, hard days lay ahead but I am with you. I will walk beside you at all times. Keep you eyes focused upon me at all times. The enemy will come in to deceive you many times. I will give you strength and wisdom to come against him. I will call your husband home soon, very soon. I will send help to guide you through those days. You will have peace and strength beyond your understanding. Your boys will be great strength and support to you also, they will amaze you. Your family will stand with you and fill your needs

NEGLECTED AND FORGOTTEN 10-12-10

As we walk through the garden gate it appears as a cold fall wintery day. The flowers are droopy and some tattered and torn, but when you look deeper you see some brightly shining and standing strong and tall.

Another area they all look so beaten down: no more hope! The water in the fountain has become muddied and unclean.

Oh lord, so much needs attention and cleaning, preparing the ground for the coming spring. So much debris and dead plants. So much work to be done. It has been so neglected to get this way.

Jesus replied: yes, my child, this is what is happening around the world. Hopelessness. People are falling away from their faith, people aren't caring for and building up their brothers and sisters. Many have turned to man and away from the father. Some have completely fallen into the darkness I promised never to leave nor forsake them, to supply their needs, for them to wait upon me, but they grew weak and weary, and no one came to lift them up and encourage them back on the right road. Yes, there is much work that must be done. My people that truly serve me, with deep intercession and spreading the gospel tending to their needs and their souls.

Many can be restored but many have already chosen the other path.

The work ahead is heavy and the days is short, but the time is never too late: for together the land can be healed, with much prayer and supplications the muddied waters can be made clean and pure once again psl 81

THE SEASON IS LATE 10-22-10

As we walk into the garden: the season is late fall. The flowers are dying back, the trees have dropped most of their leaves covering the ground to protect the plants for the coming wintery days ahead. Some birds are scampering about searching for food to fatten for the coming winter months. But wait I hear cheeps of disparity all around me. No those aren't chirps of joy, no those are cheeps of a different kind: help. Or lame, broken legs or wings: they can't forge for themselves as the others so they are doomed to perish. As we walk through the fields of dying flowers and chirping birds, Jesus reaches his hand out and the lame and hurting birds are healed. He calls them his flock. He doesn't speak to them individually just points them out as we slowly walk by them. Each one jumps away as it is healed and begins to search for food as the others.

Jesus says: these are, as, many of my children as around the world. They too are lame and suffering as their spirits are sick and need a healing word. As I don't want any to perish when my father calls his children to the marriage supper table. Psl 4

Printed in the United States
by Baker & Taylor Publisher Services